122.7 million

151.6 million

1 9 3 0

1 9 4 0

1940
President Roosevelt's
third term;
Mount Rushmore
completed

1930
The Great Depression;
Dust Bowl;
President
Herbert Hoover

1941
Pearl Harbor;
declaration of war
on Japan;
Axis powers
declare war on U.S.;
early TV;
Joe DiMaggio

1927
Charles A. Lindbergh
flight in
The Spirit of St. Louis;
Babe Ruth—
60 homers
in one season

1931
Will Rogers

1932
President
Franklin D. Roosevelt

1942
Generals
Douglas MacArthur
and
Dwight Eisenhower

1933
New York Mayor
Fiorello H. LaGuardia

1934
Repeal of
Prohibition

1929
Wall Street
crash

1939
Outbreak of
World War II
in Europe

1943
Winston Churchill;
General
George S. Patton;
D day at Normandy

1935
DC–3 introduced by
American Airlines

1937
Opening of the
Golden Gate Bridge

1938
Fascism,
Benito Mussolini;
Nazism,
Adolph Hitler

1945
President
Harry S. Truman;
A-bombs dropped
on Japan; end of
World War II

THIS *Incredible* CENTURY

Photo credit: Catherine Noren

This Incredible Century

NORMAN VINCENT PEALE

Tyndale House Publishers, Inc.
WHEATON, ILLINOIS

Library of Congress Cataloging-in-Publication Data

Peale, Norman Vincent, 1898-
    This incredible century / Norman Vincent Peale.
        p.   cm.
    Includes index.
    ISBN 0-8423-4615-5
    1. Peale, Norman Vincent, 1898-   2. Reformed Church in
America—Clergy—Biography.   3. Reformed Church—United States—
Clergy—Biography.   4. Twentieth century. I. Title.
BX9543.P4A3   1991
285.7'092—dc20   90-72126
[B]

Timeline photo credits:
H. Armstrong Roberts—Masked, hooded gunman; Statue of
Liberty; Mt. Rushmore; Charles Lindbergh; Wright aeroplane;
Prince Charles, Princess Diana; Adolph Hitler. *H. Sutton/
H. Armstrong Roberts*—The Brandenburg Gate.
UPI/Bettman Newsphotos—The Beatles; Babe Ruth.
UPI/Bettman— Elvis Presley. *The Bettman Archive*—The
Titanic; Model T Ford; Atomic bomb mushroom; Uncle Sam
poster. *NASA*—Astronaut Edwin Aldrin; Spaceship
Challenger. *FPG International*—Helicopter. *United
Media*—Peanuts cartoon.

98   97   96   95   94   93   92
 9   8   7   6   5   4

CONTENTS

ACKNOWLEDGMENTS

I am indebted to the following people and sources:

Sybil Light, my secretary, who typed and retyped this manuscript and who made invaluable suggestions.

John M. Allen, who edited much of this material.

Philip L. Carret, for stock market research.

Bill Kieran, automobile dealer of Pawling, New York, for information regarding early cars.

Wendell Hawley, senior vice president of Tyndale House Publishers, who suggested the idea of this book and who helped in its organization.

Virginia Muir, who gave this manuscript the final professional editing.

Chronicle of America (Mount Kisco, N.Y.: Chronicle Publications, Inc., 1989), which provided many helpful details regarding historical events.

Treasury of Early American Automobiles by Floyd Clymer (New York: Bonanza Books, 1950).

The Timetables of History: A Horizontal Linkage of People and Events by Bernard Grun (New York: Simon and Schuster, 1987).

The Timetable of Technology: A Record of Our Century's Achievements, Patrick Harpur, ed. (London: Michael Joseph Limited, 1982).

INTRODUCTION

THIS was a wonderful country at the turn of the twentieth century, simple and homey, yet already bursting with the excitement of an incredible future. Most of it was rural with small towns, fertile farmland, dusty (or muddy) one-lane roads stretching between villages. Brick or frame farmhouses were surrounded by gigantic trees, indicating the richness of the soil, which produced ample living for most farmers. Cities seemed far away and for the most part were overgrown small towns, except for a few centers where big money financed a sophisticated society.

But for all that, in the last years of the nineteenth century and for twenty years of the twentieth century, America was still a horse-and-buggy civilization. In the cities, as well, transportation was by horse-drawn vehicles, though some were more ornate than in the country. Even streetcars came lumbering along pulled by sturdy horses. The day of the horseless carriage had not yet arrived.

The author of this chronicle was born in a typical small village on the 31st of May 1898, one year and seven months before the twentieth century came in on a frosty night, joyously welcomed by all future-minded citizens. America was just coming of age, and people everywhere from East to West and North to South were sure we were entering a great new era. Ancient wrongs would be righted, everyone would be educated, poverty would be no more, true brotherhood would reign, a bright future loomed. The golden age was upon us.

I have returned occasionally to the house where I was born. The nice people who now live there have every modern convenience, including radio, TV, and VCR. But I arrived that night by the light of an oil lamp. I was delivered by my own father, an M.D. turned preacher, without the aid of a trained nurse, just a couple of local women who usually helped at the birth of a baby. The house was heated by coal stoves, and meals were cooked on a wood-burning range—but such delicious meals, and all the baked goods came from those old stoves.

Many revolutionary inventions were just ahead. Alexander Graham Bell had recently invented an instrument called by the strange name of "telephone." Then Thomas A. Edison, a man with a gifted brain, after some five thousand failed experiments finally invented an incandescent bulb that worked, and he called it an electric light. Meanwhile, up in Detroit a strange man was tinkering in his barn with a machine in which, it was rumored, you could ride without being pulled by a horse.

Soon came plumbing whereby one could wash dishes and clothes in a "sink" and have flush toilets, thus doing away with the privy out back where one nearly froze on a winter night. Now you could have a bath in a permanent tub in a room called a bathroom. Gone was the tin washtub in the kitchen, where Americans had bathed for decades.

Later came the motion picture, another offspring of the creative mind of Thomas A. Edison, who had also invented the gramophone, later called a Victrola.

We were not satiated by one wonder after another, but excited by all of them. Was not America one country that marched to a strain no country in history had ever equaled? Was not the United States of America the greatest country in the history of the world? So most of us thought and believed.

And now years later—though perhaps wiser, more philosophical, a bit more sophisticated—I still preserve the opinion I had in my youth. This is even yet a great land of freedom and is still what Lincoln once called "the last best hope of earth."

I personally know how things were during the twentieth century, for I lived through it all. Even the "primitive" life was not all that bad. Indeed it was wonderful: It was life that *was* life. Perhaps I'm overly sentimental about days that are gone and will not come back, for even as I write about those halcyon days of youth, tears form in my eyes.

In the chapters of this book I want to tell about the America I knew personally, the America that was to become the America that is. It is now on its way to becoming the America that is to be. My nine decades of life as a native-born American are, I feel, an unforgettable and exciting story. I am eager to tell about the country where life that is life is still within the reach of every American.

CHAPTER 1

How
I Remember
the First
Decade

THIS panorama of an exciting life spanning nine decades began just nineteen months before the end of the nineteenth century. Actually, looking back, I seem to remember a few great events at the start of that period, one being the disaster of the battleship *Maine*, which was blown up in Havana harbor on February 15, 1898. Another was Teddy Roosevelt leading his Rough Riders in an exciting charge up San Juan Hill on July 1 of the same year.

I realize that the first of these unforgettable events happened some three and a half months before my birth and the second only a month afterward, so I could have no personal memories of either. However, the audacity of the Spaniards in sinking a ship of the United States Navy so inflamed the American populace that they angrily talked about it for several years afterward. I, and indeed every youngster of that era, listened, wide-eyed; and it sank so deeply into my consciousness that in effect, if not in fact, it formed a lifelong "memory."

The indomitable, fearless, dashing TR, idol of those days, formed a troop of daredevils called "Rough Riders." I recall my father telling me he had wanted to go with Teddy Roosevelt and his Rough Riders.

"Why didn't you, Dad?" I wanted to know.

"Because of you," he replied rather sadly, I thought. "I couldn't leave your young pregnant mother, now could I?"

Two and a half years after my birth my brother Robert Clifford was born, and from then on we were inseparable. My second brother, Leonard Delaney, was born much later, in 1912. We lived in Cincinnati with our mother, Anna, and our preacher-doctor father, Charles Clifford Peale.

Compared with today's life-style the decade 1900 to 1910 was simple, to some extent even primitive, but, like most children, I personally remember the time as fun, constantly interesting, even exciting. Memories of this decade are pleasant ones.

Let me tell you a few things we did not have. We had no electric lights in the house, indeed no electric power. Perhaps some of the rich of that period might have been able to afford this newfangled invention, but we who lived in Cincinnati had natural gas for lighting. I recall that we had to go around at night carefully turning off the gas lamps, smelling the fixture to be sure no gas was escaping to asphyxiate us in the night. All meals were cooked on a coal or wood-burning stove. But let me tell you, I will stack those meals against today's cooking any day: tasty, fragrant, healthful, with fresh food from gardens or nearby farms, simply and well cooked.

In the summer we went by train to Grandma and Grandpa Peale's home at Lynchburg in Highland County, Ohio, about fifty miles from Cincinnati. Here life was really simple, inno-cent, and great fun. We relied on coal oil lamps, and I can visualize Grandma, glasses down her nose, reading the *Chris-tian Advocate* by sputtering lamplight. Then when she said, "Boys, time for bed," she would pick up the lamp to lead the way toward the back door and into darkness. Bob and I, half scared, would follow as she lit our way out to the privy back by the barn. There were no indoor toilets, no bathtubs, not even running water.

Back at the house we would follow her upstairs, glancing nervously at the shadows. We'd change into our nightshirts and jump into a huge four-poster bed that had been in the family since the 1760s. Grandma would tuck us in, hear our brief prayers, and offer one of her own: "Dear Lord, watch over these little boys tonight and bring them safe to morning light." And then she would say, "Good night, sleep tight." We lay there listening to her footsteps retreating down the stairs. The lamplight, briefly reflected on the wall, disappeared, leaving us to snuggle together in the darkness and silence. But soon, having run around all day, we were quickly in what Grandma picturesquely called "God's sleepy land."

If, in the night, nature had to be served, there was a "chamber" under the bed, a china pot. A larger china receptacle, which had a lid, reposed in the corner, and into this the contents of the "chamber" were put.

Grandpa had not piped water into the house, but some of the sweetest, purest water I've ever tasted was drawn from a well outside the kitchen door. A pitcher filled with this water and a large bowl in the bedroom made washing a pleasure on warm summer mornings. But it became a rather heroic ordeal when, on winter visits, we found it necessary to break the ice to perform our morning ablutions. I recall how it made the blood race in my veins as I ran downstairs to warm at least one side of myself at the big base burner stove in the parlor where Grandpa had a coal fire going. You could see it blazing behind the isinglass on the stove front.

While we are on such mundane subjects, I must mention the Saturday night baths. No one in those days ever took a bath except on Saturday night. That was so you would be respectable at Sunday school and church the next morning. (And some people didn't bathe at all in the winter, fearing colds or pneumonia.) The bath ritual was the same, whether in our Cincinnati home or at Lynchburg. After Saturday night supper, usually baked beans with salt pork and brown bread, a big, oval-shaped boiler filled with well water would be heated on the coal range in the kitchen. Large pails filled with cold water sat on the floor. You would undress and ladle hot water into a washtub doubling as a bathtub, tempering it with the cold water. Then, having stepped in and become wet, you would proceed to soap your body. Next, standing in the washtub, you would pour tempered water over yourself, step out of the tub, have a brisk rubdown, don a bathrobe, and scamper into the parlor for family prayers.

And the family prayers were, indeed, unforgettable. We all knelt down in the parlor, a room never used except for a funeral or a visit by the pastor or some other special purpose, like our evening prayers. To begin with, Grandma always prayed first, and she was not, shall I say, succinct. In fact, her prayers were prolonged. She told the Lord all about everything, including us. At times she seemed to be pleading with God, at other times she appeared to be arguing with the Almighty. She preferred to call it "wrestling with God," reminiscent of Jacob's anguish in Genesis, chapter 32. If wrestling was the right term, Bob and I felt the Lord had a competent adversary on His hands.

We were kneeling at what they used to call "horsehair" furniture, very formal divans, couches, and chairs upholstered in a stiff black covering. Fidgety youngsters down on their knees could with their little fingers get hold of the ends of horsehairs and ease them out. Pulling the hairs up during many a long prayer, I often wondered how any remained in the furniture.

Sometimes I used to ask myself, *Were those family prayers really meaningful?* Years later I found the answer. My Uncle Will, much younger than my father, Clifford, and not a pious man or regular churchgoer, was ill in Memorial Hospital in

New York. I went to see him, and he said in a plaintive voice, taking my hand, "Pray for me, Norman, and pray just like Ma used to do."

So I tried to emulate Grandma's prayer. "Dear Lord Jesus our Savior, bless little Willie today." (She always called him Willie—that big strapping Texas oil man.) "He's just a little boy, Lord, and You said, 'Suffer the little children to come unto Me.' You love him and I'm worried about him. But You said, 'You just leave him to Me.' Now he is to be operated on. Take care of him, heavenly Father, for You know how much we all love him. In Jesus' name, amen."

Both Uncle Will and I were too broken up after this to speak. I did what I had never done to this strong he-man; I kissed him on the forehead and rumpled his hair. He reached for my hand and lovingly patted it. So those long-winded prayers of my saintly grandmother years before had taken deep root in two grown men and gave us strength years later.

After Grandma's lengthy prayer, Grandpa took over. He was a wonderful Christian, same as Grandma, but his prayers were short and to the point. Then he said, "Now, boys, it's your turn," and we each mumbled out a few sentences. Fortified with Bible reading and prayer, we had a light snack of milk and Grandma's homemade cookies, which were kept in a cookie jar conveniently placed for kids. We all sat around for awhile, until Grandma came out with her "Time for bed, boys."

The house was typical of most homes of the 1900–1910 era and well up to 1920, for that matter. Grandpa had no telephone and, of course, radio and television were far in the future. But we had the Cincinnati *Times-Star* every evening. Grandpa and Grandma got a telephone sometime after 1910. It was a large, shellacked pine, boxlike contraption hung on the wall. It had a mouthpiece speaker and a bell above.

One picked up the long black cylindrical receiver or ear

piece, which hung on one side of the box, then turned a crank on the side of the box to call "Central," the operator in the local telephone office. You would tell her the number desired. She would then connect you to your party. Usually one was on what was called a "party line," especially in the country and small towns, meaning that several subscribers were hooked together on one line, and any or all of them, if interested, could listen in on your conversation. The more people were listening in, the fainter became the voice of the person you were calling. Sometimes it became necessary to issue a general request: "Please get off the line so we can hear better!"

Actually, the first electric transmission of the human voice took place on March 10, 1876, by Alexander Graham Bell in Boston. He had been working on this device for some years. On that memorable day Bell accidentally spilled battery acid on his leg and called to his assistant, "Watson, come here. I need you." Watson, who was on another floor, heard this call clearly over the instrument and ran to help Bell, thus giving him the good news that his experiment worked at last. On June 25 of that year, at the Centennial Exposition in Philadelphia, this new invention was demonstrated, but bankers were wary of giving financial assistance for its manufacture, regarding it as a curiosity with no practical future.

My father, more progressive than our grandparents, had a telephone installed in 1907. I remember the thrill we all had when we realized we could send and receive messages by voice instead of sending someone, usually me, with a written note. This was when we lived on Gilman Avenue in Cincinnati. Like the early motor cars, the telephone did not always operate with efficiency. It developed static and sometimes did not function at all. Not many people had telephones as early as we did, and they did not come into general use for several years. I recall the inquiry, "Are you on the telephone?"

There was no refrigerator in Grandpa's house or in our home in the city. But we did have an icebox, and the ice man came by perhaps twice a week and looked at the front window, where a cardboard sign told him whether we needed twenty-five or fifty pounds of ice. He then chipped out a piece of the size desired and carried the block into the kitchen to fit it into the icebox top. We kids were permitted to go for the small chips of ice on the man's wagon, which we sucked contentedly. A pan had to be placed under the icebox to collect the melting ice water, and we had to watch it carefully lest it overflow, which it often did.

In the winter the housewife who did not have an icebox put perishables—meat, milk, butter, eggs and the like—inside the door of the parlor, which was seldom heated. In the summer she might put perishables down into the well; milk and butter were usually delivered daily from a farmer or the local cream-ery. I can recall the milk in open pails and the butter, not shaped into blocks as now, in open crocks. The milk, of course, was not homogenized, nor could you order the low-fat variety. It had plenty of cream on top. At that time milk cost twenty-six cents a gallon, and eggs were twenty cents a dozen; five pounds of flour cost fourteen cents.

Air-conditioning was a convenience of the future. Indeed, until the fourth decade of the twentieth century we never heard of it. We used medium-sized paper fans with a wooden stick handle, waving them vigorously by hand to stir up the air and fend off flies. The fans were usually supplied by the local undertaker, and his advertisement was displayed in large letters on both sides, sometimes accompanied by a colorful landscape photograph. Congregations in church on hot Sundays endured the heat thanks to these undertakers' fans. And all windows were wide open. We used to joke that all the flies in Ohio were religiously inclined, so many of them came to church.

The heat in those days was terrible. I remember one terrifically hot day in August on a train running between Indianapolis and Cincinnati. Every window was open, through which came the ubiquitous flies as well as smoke and cinders from the engine up ahead. The parlor car in which I was riding was one of the hottest places I've encountered in my life, despite the futile efforts of the fans at either end. A fat man, with perspiration running down his face, which he was wiping constantly with a big linen handkerchief, observed: "It's as hot as hell." Since I had never been there, I didn't know quite how to make a comparison, but agreed with him on the basis of what I had heard about hell.

This was decades before the day of casual dress. The man across the aisle was wearing a jacket and a white shirt with a stiff detachable collar (the kind through which you inserted brass buttons front and back to attach to the shirt). All this was the fashion of those days, both in club cars and in day coaches as well. Fashion dictated that men should always wear jackets. A baseball game on a hot day may have been an exception. Even then the coat, if removed, would be laid carefully across the knees and put back on immediately after the game ended.

The heat experienced in the "good old summertime" of the early decades of this century disturbed me so much that when interviewed years later by a Chicago newspaper reporter who asked what I considered the greatest invention ever to come from the ingenious mind of man, I instantly responded, "air-conditioning."

But summer was not always as bad as the foregoing would seem to indicate. We had open streetcars in Cincinnati, which were a joy to ride for a nickel fare. These are seen no longer, more's the pity, for they were delightful. What a breeze they worked up going along Gilbert Avenue or running along Montgomery Pike in Norwood on a summer day! The conductor somewhat perilously made his way along an outside running board, holding onto stanchions while he collected and rang up fares and handed out transfers. When the car stopped, the generator beneath throbbed like a racer getting its breath. But as the car began to move again, we felt that life-giving breeze sweep through the car. This was before automobile traffic. Only horse-drawn carriages, drays, and delivery wagons from local stores were in the streets.

Occasionally, Mother and Father would take us for a ride up and down one of the inclined planes that transported passengers on some of the hills of Queen City. A streetcar would run onto a waiting platform, which was attached to a cog railway mechanism that carried the car up and down. It was long an interesting feature of Cincinnati in the early decades of this century and was reminiscent of some European cities.

Then there was the unforgettable *Island Queen*, a beautiful steamboat that plied the Ohio River from Cincinnati to Coney Island and return, a distance of about ten miles. I do not recall the round-trip fare, but I doubt that it was more than a quarter for adults and fifteen cents for children under twelve. Ice cream cones cost a nickel and so did a big bag of popcorn. I remember the roller coaster at Coney Island where you held on tightly for the breathtaking steep ascents and downward swoops. And one attraction I shall never forget was called "The Maze," a confused series of passageways where you ran into yourself in mirrors placed at every turn.

Occasionally, Father would take us to baseball games to see our idols, the Cincinnati Reds. There we saw some notables of the era, like the immortal pitchers Christy Mathewson and Cy Young.

For years I have heard a touching story about Babe Ruth. I've talked about this story with Branch Rickey, one of the greatest authorities on baseball, and he attested to its validity. It is certainly true to the Babe's nature.

The story goes that in the twilight of his unparalleled career, Babe Ruth was playing in Cincinnati. He was now striking out more often than getting hits and actually committed errors. It became so bad that sometimes the great Babe Ruth was actually booed by the fans. On one such occasion the Babe, head on chest, was dejectedly walking toward the dugout amidst derisive booing when suddenly a small boy, tears running down his face, ran unhindered out on the field and threw his arms around Babe's legs. Ruth, who always had a big heart for kids, reached down and took the boy into his big arms. He talked with him as they continued to the dugout. Silence fell over the packed stands. The booing ceased. So moved were the fans that simultaneously they stood silently in ultimate tribute, as the great athlete and a little boy passed in one of the most affecting episodes of the American game.

In Lynchburg, where Bob and I spent every summer, was one of the first movie houses, called "picture shows" in those days. It was the period of the silent picture. Talking pictures came a few decades later. I have the recollection that admission was a dime. Popcorn and peanuts were on sale for a nickel a bag.

Silent and primitive as the pictures were, they were exciting nonetheless. A pounding piano player closely followed the mood and action on the screen. For example, when the hero was racing on horseback to rescue the maiden, or the blue-clad troops were dashing to overcome an Indian raid, the pianist would speed up until the audience would shout, "Go get 'em, soldier boys." The picture lasted less than an hour. There were no afternoon shows except on Saturday, when many farm families were in town. And, of course, no movies were shown on the Sabbath.

On summer Saturday nights in Lynchburg we attended band concerts on the green and heard old Civil War favorites like "Tenting Tonight on the Old Camp Ground" and hymns like

"When the Roll Is Called Up Yonder." The concert ended about ten o'clock with a patriotic song, during which all removed hats and the old veterans stood with hands over their hearts.

One of the great days of the year was May 30, "Decoration Day," so placed in the yearly calendar because spring flowers were in bloom. It was then that the Women's Relief Corps, founded during the Civil War, decorated the graves of veterans.

In the afternoon of Decoration Day (later called Memorial Day) a parade of the old Civil War veterans, dressed in blue uniforms, marched to the village cemetery, then to a pasture nearby where a platform had been erected and folding chairs from the undertakers and churches were set up to accommodate a big crowd. Some locally famous speaker would orate about the "recent rebellion" and praise the dead and the living Civil War veterans.

On one such occasion I was seated between Grandpa and Grandma. Bob was next to Mother. Father was on the platform, where he had delivered the Memorial Day sermon. A local politician of the county was orator of the day. He was a spellbinder. He was waxing especially eloquent in describing the heroic exploits of the soldiers, when suddenly his false teeth flew out and landed in the sawdust right near me. Grandma hurriedly said, "Norman, pick up those teeth and hand them to the speaker." I didn't very much want to touch his false teeth, but prodded by Grandma, seconded by Mother, I gingerly picked them up and handed them up to the speaker, who clamped them in place and went on with his speech.

We had good times those summers in Lynchburg. There were hayrides when Bob and I, with our first cousins who lived in Lynchburg—Philip and Howard Henderson, Nell, Noreen, Marion, Edwin, and Lewis Delaney, Ada and Dorothy Decker—would pile onto the wagon heaped high with hay.

Two horses in tandem drew the wagon, driven by a man with a long whip used as much to keep the horseflies off the horses as to hasten them along.

We would go about three miles into the country to a farmhouse where we would have a huge dinner and then drive back, singing songs in the moonlight.

Each summer some boys in the town would wait for us two city boys from Cincinnati, threatening to beat us up. But with all our cousins to support us, they never did succeed. A couple of years ago I met one of those Lynchburg boys in Chicago. He is now a well-known retired Chicago businessman. This time instead of beating me up he affectionately embraced me as an old friend! Thus time changes attitudes.

My father, a prominent pastor in Cincinnati, was a friendly, outgoing man who seemed to know everyone. He built the Grace Methodist Episcopal Church in Norwood, an independent suburb of Cincinnati. Later he was pastor of the Westwood Methodist Episcopal Church in Cincinnati, and one of his loyal members was Harley Procter, chief corporate sales manager for Procter and Gamble. One Sunday my father read from Psalm 45: "All thy garments smell of myrrh, and aloes, and cassia, out of the ivory palaces. . . ." Mr. Gamble once told our family that upon hearing that psalm he immediately knew the name for the new soap he was manufacturing. He would call it Ivory Soap, "99 and 44/100 percent pure."

My father also knew William Howard Taft, the only man to be both president of the United States and chief justice of the Supreme Court. Dad always introduced me to people like this, for he wanted to give me the privilege of knowing distinguished persons. I remember that at about ten years of age I shook hands with Mr. Taft, a huge man physically. He was very kind in turning the conversation to the level of a young boy.

Mother also looked for opportunities to expose us to exceptional people. Moreover, she was likely to favor Democratic personalities, while Father was an independent Republican. One evening Mother, reading the Cincinnati *Times-Star*, spoke up. "Clifford, it says here that William Jennings Bryan is speaking at the Lancaster campgrounds on Saturday afternoon. He is to give his famous lecture on 'The Prince of Peace.' I think we ought to take the boys and attend that lecture. It says a special train will leave the station and return after the lecture." Lancaster is 30 miles from Columbus, about 120 miles from Cincinnati, and the price must have been excursion rate or my parents could not have afforded such a trip.

Early Saturday morning we boarded the train of day coaches. Soon, to our surprise, Mr. Bryan with two men, presumably bodyguards, came in and took seats, marked Reserved, across the aisle. Father, with his outgoing nature, soon engaged Bryan in conversation. A crowd of men gathered around, and Father called me to join the group. Bryan noticed the young boy in the crowd and asked, "Your son, Dr. Peale?" Surprisingly, he asked me to sit on his knee, and for several minutes he talked to me alone, asking about my interests and activities. He said, "Always be a good Christian boy," and gave me other good advice. From that moment on I became an ardent admirer of this great personality.

His lecture on "The Prince of Peace," delivered to a vast crowd, was a masterpiece and entirely nonpolitical. He was, in my opinion, probably the greatest public speaker I have ever heard. He had a strong, resonant voice and could project it with clarity to big crowds numbering into the thousands, long before we had any sound systems. His gestures were completely natural, and he had an almost magical effect on an audience with his tight and rational reasoning and especially by his obvious Christian faith. His most famous speech, "The Cross of Gold," was delivered at the Democratic national convention in Chicago on July 8, 1896, and it won him his first presidential nomination.

Once, years later, I heard him speak before a big audience in Brooklyn, where I was living. On the platform was a table with a large pitcher of water and a glass. During his talk, which, as usual, held his hearers spellbound, he walked to this table and picked up the heavy pitcher in his right hand, holding the glass in his left. Continuing a cascade of inspired speech, he lifted the pitcher at least two feet. The audience watched spellbound as he poured a stream of water into the glass, not spilling a drop, then lifted it to his mouth and drank it all at once, without missing a syllable in his speech. It was the sort of dramatic interlude for which he was famous.

Once at Greenville, Ohio, I heard him when he drew such a large crowd that the meeting was held in a pasture. The only thing readily available for a platform was a manure spreader. He mounted it and with a perfectly straight face declaimed, "Friends and fellow citizens, in my long career I have spoken from many platforms. But this is the first time" (glancing down at the manure spreader) "that I have ever spoken firmly standing on the Republican platform." The audience roared.

I never knew anyone who loved people more genuinely than my father. He was quick to respond in any case of human need. Once, when he came home late one winter day, Mother reported a request to call a certain telephone number. When he telephoned, it proved to be what was bluntly called in those days a "whorehouse," in the red-light district.

The madam told my father that one of her girls was desperately ill and that the physician had said she would hardly last the night. The girl had requested "a pastor to come and pray with me." She reported that the sick girl passed in and out of consciousness and in lucid moments repeated her desire to have a pastor pray with her. The madam said, "I do not know any pastor, but once on a Sunday night I slipped in and sat in a rear pew of your church and went out quickly at the end of the service, so I knew your name. I decided to call you, for I think of you as a kindly and understanding person." Dad said he would come at once.

Father hung up, described the situation to Mother, and then said, "Norman, put on your overcoat and come with me on a pastoral errand of mercy."

"Clifford! You are not going to take our ten-year-old son into that place of sin!" Mother gasped.

"Yes, Anna, for Norman can see Jesus Christ reaching for one of His sheep who is lost but wants to come home to the Father's house. Besides, in a place like that, what better protection can a man have than his own young son?"

At the house, with its red light above the door, we were conducted to a room where a pathetic young woman of about nineteen lay, desperately ill. My father, who had been a doctor of medicine before entering the ministry, immediately saw evidences of advanced dissolution.

"I'm a bad girl, Reverend," she said, "but my family are godly people, and I was raised a Christian and attended Sunday school. I was baptized by our good preacher. But I've brought shame on my Ma and Pa," she said in a low sad voice, stating again, "I'm a bad girl."

"No, not a bad girl, but a good girl who has been acting badly," Father said, taking her small white hand in his big strong one. "What is your name?" he asked gently.

"Mary," she replied.

"Do you love Jesus, Mary, and do you believe He will forgive your sins and wash them all away so you are whiter than snow in your soul?"

"Yes," Mary whispered.

"And do you give your soul, your whole self to the Lord, asking for salvation?"

Again, "Yes," adding, "I ask the Lord to save my soul."

Father then said, "I say to you that you are saved." Opening his Bible, he read from John, chapter 14, "Let not your heart be troubled: ye believe in God, believe also in me. In my Father's house are many mansions: if it were not so, I would have told you. I go to prepare a place for you. And if I go and prepare a place for you, I will come again and receive you unto myself; that where I am, there ye may be also."

Closing the book, he prayed a most beautiful prayer in his strong, compassionate voice.

I noted that the women of the house, who were standing along the wall, were weeping openly. That night I saw the mercy, the compassion, and the glory of the ministry as my strong, believing, kindhearted father led a mixed-up, repentant human being back to God. Later we learned that she died quietly and peacefully a few hours later. The realization that a believer, like my father, had the privilege of bringing men and women to the Lord was a determining factor in my becoming a minister.

In those far-off days, we did not have any newscasters on radio and television telling us nightly how bad everything was. The general opinion and belief was that America had an incredible future, that it was the greatest country in history. The press, in news columns and editorials, actively supported the concept that the United States was marching forward. Papers reported exciting events in the making.

By 1900 the population of the United States had increased, much of it through immigration, to 75.9 million. The Brownie Camera stimulated a craze for photography and sold for a dollar. The first "panic" of the new century hit Wall Street May 9, 1901, causing the stock exchange to close for the first time in its history. But recovery was quick. Henry Ford formed his Ford Motor Company in 1903. Enrico Caruso, in his debut at the Metropolitan Opera, was given only fair reviews. Kate Douglas Wiggin wrote *Rebecca of Sunnybrook Farm*, and Jack London wrote *The Call of the Wild.*

Sears, Roebuck and Co. in the fall "consumers guide" for 1900, advertised: "Novelty of the season: stylish plush capes appliqued with satin, the very newest thing and copied from an imported garment. 125 inches in length, $9.95." "Ladies tailor-made suit made of all-wool cheviot serge, $12.50." "Men's suits. Gunther's fancy imported dark plaid German worsted cloth in suits to measure, $12.50." "Men's winter flannel shirts, $1.00." "Overcoats, $11.00."

On December 17, 1903, at Kitty Hawk, North Carolina, the Wright Brothers tossed a coin to decide which would be the first to fly their 750-pound gasoline-powered plane. Orville won, climbed aboard dressed in his usual white starched shirt with necktie and jacket, and flew a distance of 120 feet for twelve seconds, thus inaugurating a worldwide industry that wrought a basic revolution in transportation.

Ice cream cones were invented at the St. Louis World's Fair in 1904. They proved the old saying "necessity is the mother of invention." A Syrian immigrant, Ernest Hamuri, ran out of dishes at his ice cream stand. He rolled a Persian pastry called zalabria into a cone-shaped holder. It caught on and continues to be one of the nation's most popular treats.

October 27, 1904, marked the first day of the New York subway, which ran from City Hall to Harlem in fifteen minutes, at a nickel a ride. A passenger reported the theft of a five-hundred-dollar pin, which reminds us that things haven't changed much. The first meeting of the Rotary International was held in Chicago on February 23, 1905. Just before dawn on April 18, 1906, in six consecutive shocks, a gigantic earthquake and the resulting fires leveled San Francisco. Over one thousand persons were killed, and newspaper reports sent by telegraph said,

"The financial loss is beyond computation."

So it went through the decade, one tragic or interesting event after another in an exciting era. The forward pass was made legal in 1906 in an attempt to reduce the number of injuries and fatalities in college football. A hand-cranked washing machine, invented in the 1850s, was converted to operate by electricity, which had been discovered and harnessed by Thomas A. Edison in 1879. Oklahoma became the forty-sixth state November 16, 1907, and in 1908 the electric iron and the electric toaster reached America's housewives.

William Howard Taft, who was elected in 1908, became president on March 4, 1909. Admiral Peary reached the North Pole the same year, and "Memphis Blues" was created by W. C. Handy in 1909.

On August 12, 1908, the famed Model T Ford came out, with a twenty-horsepower engine. Henry Ford himself drove the first car through the streets of Detroit and said the company would sell twenty-five thousand of them next year. The Model T sold for $850. My father later bought a secondhand one for $400, which was more like it for a preacher's wallet.

I met the legendary Henry Ford only once. It was when I was a newspaper reporter in Detroit in 1921. Coming out of the Detroit railroad station, I saw a man standing beside a car and I recognized him as Henry Ford. He was looking at a piece of paper that he held in his hand. In the front seat of the car was a woman I recognized as Mrs. Ford.

I walked over and said, "Mr. Ford, I may never have this opportunity again and I admire you so much. I would just like to shake your hand." He extended his hand and asked what I did. I told him I worked on a newspaper.

He then asked me a seemingly irrelevant question. "Who is your best friend?" Without waiting for my answer, he tore off a ragged piece from the paper he was holding and wrote with a pencil, "Your best friend is the person who brings out the best that is within you," and signed it "Henry Ford."

He then said, "Think about that and always associate with the best men you know." With a wave he got into his car and drove off. For a long time I kept that piece of paper on which he wrote those wise words, but over the years it has disappeared, much to my loss.

I lost another paper, upon which Governor Nelson Rockefeller wrote something I prized. We were fellow speakers at a Rotary assembly in the Grand Ballroom of the Waldorf-Astoria in New York in 1979. There were some two thousand Rotarians from New York, New Jersey, and Connecticut in the audience. I spoke first, followed by Nelson, and he made his usual charming speech, greeting the big audience of men with his usual salutation, "Hi, fellas!"

Finishing the speech he returned to his seat beside mine. I said, "Terrific speech. You're something special."

He said, "Give me your program." He wrote something on it. I remember clearly what it was. It was supergenerous, but he was that kind of man. He had written, "To Norman Peale, who has done more good for more people than any man alive. Affectionately, Nelson."

He then stood up, patted me on the back and shook my hand saying, "I must go. Be seein' you." But I never did see him again, for he died suddenly about two weeks later, on January 25, 1979. He was one of our greatest governors and a lovable personality.

The automobile was practically unknown in 1895. Ten years later it was a hundred-million-dollar business. In 1895 the "factory" was a barn, the equipment a drill press and a lathe. Ten years later the cows were driven from the barns and an assembly line took their place.

In 1895 pioneer inventors of the automobile were exploring

steam and electricity as well as gasoline for fuel. Actually, electric-powered cars were built as far back as the 1880s. Some of my friends' families had electric-powered cars. They were quiet, even elegant. When the emphasis began to be put on speed, the electric cars gradually lost their appeal.

The early gasoline-powered cars, motorized buggies really, made all kinds of noise as they rattled and bounced over the rutted, dusty roads of that time. This was a reason that twenty-five well-known companies manufactured electric-powered cars. The ads said, "Clean, quiet, stylish, and easy to operate—the only car for a lady." They were on the market until 1915-17. The last electric car company, "Detroit Electric," still made cars on order in the 1930s.

I remember driving in 1918 with Charles B. Mills, a fellow student at Ohio Wesleyan University, from Delaware, Ohio, to nearby Marysville in an electric car belonging to his family. To negotiate the twenty miles between those towns required most of an afternoon. It was a closed car with richly upholstered seats and beautiful, decorative features. I recall that for every battery the electric charge would develop approximately fifteen horse-power hours.

For a long time, sturdy, dependable cars were being made, yet the prejudice against automobiles continued. A 1940 city ordinance in Kansas City required four qualifications of motorists: skill, experience, capacity, and sobriety. We might do well to revive those requirements, what with the prevalence of drunken driving. "I prefer the dependable horse," some people said. In Pennsylvania there was an organization called "The Farmers Anti-Automobile Society," and members were said to be encouraged to patrol the roads and shout at motorcar drivers. In Fort Worth, Texas, any person riding or driving a horse could, merely by putting up his hands, cause the car to stop until the horse had passed. I recall that such a custom prevailed in southern Ohio during my boyhood. I do not believe it was an ordinance, simply a custom developed out of the antipathy against the motorcar at the time.

My friend Bill Kieran, motorcar dealer in Pawling, New York, brought me books that present the foregoing and other interesting facts about early motorcars: *Those Wonderful Old Automobiles* and *Treasury of Early American Automobiles* by Floyd Clymer.

I well recall people yelling at stranded motorists, "Get a horse," and I, who have grown up along with the motorcar, still wonder at the efficiency of modern cars that run for months without the necessity of repairs. I go back in memory to the days of planetary transmission, when you had to adjust the magneto, which produced the spark to ignite the engine, and then run around the car and crank it. If the spark didn't catch, you had to run back to adjust the magneto, then run back to crank it again. But when you got the car going after these athletic activities and were bowling along, you might say "bouncing," it was great fun. I remember even yet the smooth purr of the motor along country roads, the floorboards rattling, driving over covered bridges, meeting cars, and, if the road was narrow, turning out in a wide place. It was fun, even so, and I would not for the world have missed the exciting days of early motoring in southern Ohio.

General Motors was formed on September 14, 1908, and plans were set in motion, said a newspaper, to compete against Ford with sleek styling. Cars in the first and second decades of this century were quite unlike the sleek, well-appointed and well-engineered automobiles of today. They had no heaters and certainly no air-conditioning. They still had many of the aspects of the open carriages that they replaced. The tonneau or body of the automobile was open above the tops of door levels save for struts that supported the top of the vehicle, as in the old-style horse-drawn carriage.

Weather sidings, made to fit the vehicle, were provided, but these were rolled up and stored in the car trunk. Where windows would normally be, there was what was called isinglass to permit one to see out, albeit rather dimly. These weather sidings were for use in case of rain, snow, or cold. The problem was that you had to get out in the rain and struggle with the wind to get them on properly, and, to compound the misery, sometimes the snaps for attachment proved difficult.

Outside the car on either side was a running board on which one stepped to get in or out. Always a car carried blankets in which one could wrap up against the cold. Sometimes hot bricks to keep the feet warm were also provided. The many railroad crossings were not well protected by warnings of the approach of trains, so someone would have to get out of the car and look carefully both ways, up and down the tracks, before crossing.

Still, despite these seemingly adverse conditions, motoring in the simple early decades was great fun, and it vastly enlarged people's mobility and horizons.

A certain wealthy widow, Mrs. Hawes, lived in our neighborhood. She was a member of Father's church, and we called her Auntie Hawes. Her house was one of the large and imposing brick homesteads of the type still to be seen in some small towns and rural areas of the Midwest. She had one of the early Cadillacs, and on the frequent occasions when she invited our family to dinner, she would send her driver for us and later return us home.

I still remember the thrill of those rides in Auntie Hawes's Cadillac along gravel roads running between white fences, the smoothly purring motor, the swish of the tires, the elegance of the car. When with a flourish and the sounding of the musical horn we swept through the big gates and up a winding driveway flanked by gigantic trees, pulling up at the portico of Antie Hawes's home, we'd had an impressive experience.

And I've never forgotten those marvelous old-style country dinners in a great house of that era: chicken and gravy, roasting ears (as we then called corn on the cob), cornbread, mashed potatoes, ice cream and cake, pie—Ohio cooking at its best.

I determined then, as a boy, that someday in the glorious land of Sometime I would drive my own Cadillac. After a succession of lesser cars (names withheld) came the long-dreamed-of day in Cincinnati when I proudly drove my own Cadillac out of the salesroom and took the highway to my home in New York, thinking lovingly of Auntie Hawes all the way. I was still driving that car ten years later, so well was it made and so thin was my wallet.

My father was an honest, eloquent preacher. He was thoroughly committed to Christ, and he believed in people who didn't believe in themselves. As a result, he turned many lives around.

He felt that when he got people to believing in Jesus Christ and following Him faithfully, he had done the best thing that could ever be done for anyone. Accordingly, he often had in his Sunday school what he called "Decision Day." Sunday schools in those days were packed with kids and huge adult classes were popular too. Decision Day was memorable. Everyone was at the church. Father in his own wonderful way would tell the young people and adults what life with Jesus could be.

I listened and was deeply moved. I believed what Father said, and I, too, believed in Jesus. I went forward and took Dad's hand and heard him say, "This is the greatest decision you will ever make, Son." Now, about eighty years later, I would like to tell him how right he was. Although he is now in heaven, I think he knows how I feel.

One summer Sunday afternoon my father said he wanted to call on a family living a couple miles out of town in the country near Greenville, and he asked me to accompany him. We went on foot, our little fox terrier, Tip, running along with us. It was a rich countryside we traveled—Darke County, Ohio—and we passed prosperous-looking farms and waved to the people, since of course we knew them all. I recall that one family persuaded us to stop for a drink of cold lemonade, it being a warm day. The farmer's wife served us a heaping dish of home-made vanilla ice cream with cookies. I have eaten ice cream all around the world, but that dish remains in my memory as the most delectable ever—it was unforgettable.

We reached the family my father wanted to see. They were having some kind of trouble to which he brought his caring spirit and practical skills. Then we started home, and he got me talking about myself. I unloaded my problem about inferiority feelings, a low self-esteem.

My father's experience as a doctor and his genius as a pastor made him an acute curer of souls. His perception that excessive guilt from bad thoughts, or wrong thinking about personality traits, could be harmful made him adept in dealing with my inferiority complex.

Finally we came to a place where several trees had been cut down, and we sat on convenient stumps. Father described the mechanism of inferiority and self-doubt feelings in a manner that could do credit to a modern psychiatrist. He stated that scientific treatment could probably cure me, but that such treatment was not available in our little village; besides, it was quite expensive.

"But," he continued, "there is a Doctor right here who can cure any disease of the mental and emotional life. He has a rare and amazing power to curette out unhealthy thought patterns. And He can heal the sensitive self-centeredness that lies at the root of inferiority/inadequacy feelings."

Finally Father asked me, "Norman, are you willing to let this great Doctor, Jesus Christ, treat you for that inferiority complex? If you will let Him take charge of your mind, indeed your whole life, you can be freed of this misery which, if it continues, can destroy your effectiveness." I was profoundly impressed and said I would give my life into the hands of Jesus. Father told me to kneel down by the stump, and he, too, knelt. I remember that Tip came up and licked my ear, then sat beside me. Father committed me to Christ in a moving prayer.

He then asked me to tell Jesus that I was giving myself into His hands and letting go, by an act of affirmation, all my inferiority feelings. As we walked home in the gathering twilight, I felt a strange sense of peace and happiness. I was really on top of my problems. Although I had another bout with inferiority feelings during my college days, the same remedy was applied again, with the result that this self-defeating thought pattern was healed through the positive power of Jesus Christ.

I suppose I have spoken at about as many sales rallies and conventions as anyone, and I have had a lifelong interest in salesmanship and an appreciation of people in sales. In all likelihood this interest began with a sales experience during the summer vacation when I was twelve. In *The Youth's Companion*, a magazine long since defunct but widely popular among boys and girls of my generation, I read a very persuasive advertisement. It told enticingly of the profits that could be made in selling aluminum cooking utensils house to house. The ad emphasized that this was an easy job that any enterprising boy could do. "It is a cinch," the ad assured.

I showed the advertisement to my father, who encouraged me to respond to it, perhaps because he thought it would be good for me, and he lent me the fifteen dollars to purchase the kit. Along with the kit came a suggested sales talk, a sure-fire spiel that would get results every time. After a few days, I felt I had mastered the sales talk; so one morning, blithely swinging my kit, I boarded the interurban streetcar for Union City, a town just over the line in Indiana. I didn't quite have the nerve to sell in my town of Greenville.

Arriving at the outskirts of Union City, I walked by a couple of streets as I mustered up a faltering nerve. But finally I started up a street. The first house was unpainted and somewhat dilapidated, which gave me an excuse to pass it by. *They aren't progressive people and wouldn't buy this new aluminum ware*, I reasoned. The next house was quite the contrary, well painted and neat, the grass closely cut, flowers along the walk. *These people are really up-to-date*, I said to myself. *They know the best and already have aluminum ware. No use trying this place.*

Then I realized I was afraid and looking for an out. So, resolutely, I took myself in hand and, with a good old positive spirit, marched straight up to the door of the third house. Praying that no one would respond, I pressed the doorbell tentatively. The door swung open violently, and before my fear-struck eyes there appeared the biggest and most ferocious woman I'd ever seen. She stood there, glaring. In a weak voice I mumbled, "You don't want any aluminum ware, do you?"

"Of course not," she barked and slammed the door in my face.

By this time I was "tired." Telling myself that I had done a day's work, I boarded the streetcar for home, realizing I had failed completely. But I wasn't about to settle for failure, so I went to see my friend Harry. "Harry," I said, "have you ever been in the aluminum business?" When he said he hadn't, I turned my full potential sales power on him. "What," I thundered, "you've never sold aluminum ware? Boy, you are really missing the experience of your life and really good profits, too." I ended up by selling Harry a half interest in my business for $7.50. Giving him the sales talk to study, I said, "I'll meet you at the corner tomorrow morning at eight o'clock sharp. Don't be late. And we'll go back to Union City and have a terrific day selling."

Thus admonished, Harry showed up on time, carrying his share of the merchandise. At Union City we passed the street of my abject failure of the day before. "That looks like good territory," said Harry. "Let's get off and canvass this street."

"No. We'll go on to the next street. I worked that one yesterday," I explained. At the street selected I said, "Now, Harry, get this straight. You must believe you are serving the needs of housewives and you must believe in yourself. Walk right up to the door firmly, put on a big smile, and never take no for an answer. You take that side, I'll take this one."

Harry walked up his walk; I walked up mine. Harry approached his door; I approached mine. Harry rang his bell; I rang mine. And, believe me, I was fortified, for I had a partner.

After my strong and vigorous ring, the door opened slowly, and before my now-confident eyes appeared the most inoffensive little woman I had ever seen. "Madam," I said in a firm, clear voice, "I've come to do you a great favor. I have come to supply you with aluminum ware."

Weakly and very politely she asked me in and ended by signing one of the best orders I sold all summer long. Years later when I spoke in Indianapolis, an aged lady took me by the hand. "You sold me some cooking utensils long ago in Union City. I liked you, for you were young and confident and enthusiastic; and what a good salesman! Now you 'sell' the gospel with the same enthusiasm, if you don't mind my using that expression." As she turned away, she said with a smile, "Would you believe it? I still have a couple of those pots and pans."

This generation doesn't know how great Sunday was in the early years of the twentieth century. All businesses closed. There was, of course, no school, and I didn't miss it, for school was tough in those days. Teachers were highly respected, and their word was law—at school and at home. If my parents ever heard a negative word about my behavior at school, I was guaranteed a very rough time at home, perhaps with the razor strap wielded by my father. Moreover, the week was demanding, especially during the two years we lived in a German section of Cincinnati, when the classes were taught in German half the day and English the other half.

Yes, the American Sabbath was a day of rest and inspiration. It actually began on Saturday with housewives cooking for Sunday, because they felt there should not be a bit of cooking done on the Sabbath Day. They used a "fireless cooker" that kept things hot, fresh, and tasty for a long time.

Long before time for service, throngs of church-goers filled the streets. The church was often packed, with standing room only, when the first hymn was announced. There was the excitement and thrill of a great congregation. And then came the sermon. Preachers then were great orators. I was fascinated by them. Dr. Henry Jameson, Bishop Quayle, Bishop Anderson, Dr. S. Parks Cadman. These men could hold vast audiences in the hollow of their hands by their oratory. They had convictions, they were believers, and they were persuasive. They so deeply injected Christian values into the lives of the Americans who heard them that in many cases not even the so-called new morality of later years could erode it. The great preachers of my boyhood were immensely effective in nurturing the faith of the American people, and now several decades and generations later, we are still reaping the benefit of their ministries.

After church, families got together. I recall how all the older folks sat around in a circle in the yard on a Sunday afternoon, talking about the early days of the family, of the struggles they had. I remember hearing Grandpa Peale, Uncle George, Uncle

Hershel, and Uncle Lou tell how God helped them through panics and depressions when the going was hard. They were believers and strong people.

The young folks sat on the grass and listened, and faith sank into their consciousness. As a result, they tended to believe when their time came to lead families. In this way America was made great.

Mother and Father were patriotic Americans, and they wanted their boys also to love their country. For this reason they denied themselves and took us by day coach to Chicago and showed us the might of business and commerce, the throbbing life of a great city. I have loved Chicago ever since, though I never lived there. They said, "Here is the greatness of America." And at another time when an excursion at cut rates was advertised on the B & O Railroad, they took us to Washington. Father said as we toured the capital of the nation, "Here is the greatness of America."

Later, back home in Cincinnati, the family went to the village of Lynchburg, and we were invited one evening to have "supper" at a farm home. We heard the bell ring, calling the men in from the fields. They washed up outside the kitchen, using a roller towel and slicking down their hair in the mirror by the back door. Then all trooped into the dining room and quietly took seats around the table. The farmer, still dressed in overalls and holding a Bible in his big calloused hands, arose and coughed a couple of times. He read a passage. And over long years I still seem to hear the reverent voice of that good man reading the sacred words. Then, closing the Bible, the farmer turned to Father. "Brother Peale, lead us in prayer."

Later Father said thoughtfully, "We went to Chicago and Washington, looking for the greatness of America. I think we have found it here tonight."

CHAPTER 2

The Second Decade: War, Peace, and Prosperity

AS twilight came on December 31, 1909, Mother and Father were preparing for a New Year's Eve Watch Night service at the old Asbury Church in downtown Cincinnati, where my father was the pastor. He was seated at his old rolltop desk, handling accumulated correspondence.

He dipped his pen in an inkwell and, with a flourish, wrote "December 31, 1909," remarking, "That is the last time I will date a letter 1909. In a few hours we move into 1910 and go forward to a glorious future." He was right, for the decade 1910–1920 was one of the most challenging and momentous periods in our country's history. Indeed, this decade may be thought of as laying a foundation for the future.

In the spring of 1910 I viewed Halley's Comet, the greatest natural wonder I think I have ever seen. It has been more than eighty years since I saw that great comet with the eyes of youth, but I can still feel the wonder of it clearly in my memory. People were not so scientific then, and there was much fear and trembling about the comet. As a matter of fact, the comet caused thousands to panic. Comet pills were sold as an antidote for the poisonous gas it supposedly gave off. Some people expected the world to end in a shattering collision.

I was only twelve years old when Halley's Comet made its first appearance of the twentieth century. It seemed to be just above our house on Spencer Avenue in Cincinnati. What a spectacular sight it was, stretching across the sky, the head pointing toward Louisville, Kentucky, to the south and the tail toward Columbus to the north. My father explained that so exact were God's creations that the comet would return exactly 75.6 years from that night. Impressed, I said, "Gee, Dad, do you think I will be here when it comes back?"

"That isn't the important question, Son. See that you amount to something before it returns."

I was indeed here when it came back in the winter of 1985-86. But it was not at all as impressive as that 1910 visitation.

In that same year Mother decided it was time for me to have my first long pants. So she took me on the streetcar from Norwood, where we lived, to Burkhart's on Fourth Street in downtown Cincinnati to purchase a pair of long trousers. Up to that time I had been wearing knickers, as every boy did.

We walked out of the store carrying a new suit with two pairs of long pants, as was the custom at the time. Proudly I wore that new suit to church the next Sunday.

About sixty years later I was in Cincinnati on a speaking engagement, staying at the Queen City Club on Fourth Street. Going out for a walk through the old familiar streets, I passed Burkhart's store. Feeling nostalgic, I walked into the store, remembering my first long pants. Feeling I ought to buy something, I purchased a tie from the young "salesperson," as they now call them. (We used to call them "clerks.") I think I paid as much for that tie as my mother paid for my long trousers in 1910! As she wrapped my purchase, I told her about the long pants. She looked me over and commented, "Gee, that must have been a long time ago."

"Yes, ma'am, it was a long time ago, but a fellow never forgets where he bought his first long pants."

As I emerged from that store, I remembered another event on that same street, one that happened on Christmas Eve in 1910. My father had the habit of leaving his Christmas shopping to the last possible day—a habit, I admit, that was passed to his son. He and I were walking along when a tramp, dressed in ragged clothes, approached me and put a dirty hand on my arm, asking for a handout. Rudely I shook him off and the old fellow shuffled on up the street. "He's just a bum," I said to my father.

"You should never treat a man like that, Norman," Dad said, "especially on Christmas Eve." Reaching into his pocket for his thin wallet, he extracted a dollar bill. "Here, take this dollar," he said, "and go to that man and say this, 'Merry Christmas, sir. I give you this in the name of our Lord and Savior Jesus Christ.'"

"Oh, Dad, I don't want to do that," I expostulated, only to be met with a firm, "Do as I say."

Reluctantly, I caught up with the shuffling beggar and said, "Merry Christmas, sir," and, handing him the dollar bill, I added, "I give you this in the name of our Lord and Savior Jesus Christ."

A surprised look came over his face, which then broke into a smile. He removed his battered hat and with a bow said, "And Merry Christmas to you, young sir. I receive this gift in the name of our blessed Lord Jesus Christ."

Later, as we rumbled home in the streetcar, Father asked, "How did that poor old man receive your gift?"

"Why," I replied, "he was very courteous and he had a beautiful smile. He's—he's been somebody, Dad, for he acted like a gentleman."

"He still is somebody, a child of God. No one is a bum, Norman, even if he is living a bum's life. He is an immortal soul." I never forgot this incident, and I believe it affected my own lifelong respect and veneration for all people.

Well, those long pants built up my ego. One day soon after, Mother wanted to get a message to Father, who was attending a meeting downtown. "I'll take it to him," I offered.

"But you have never gone downtown on the streetcar by yourself," Mother said. "You're just a young boy, too young to go all that way alone."

"But, Mama, when you bought me those long pants, you said I was now a man. Tell you what. I'll put 'em on to take that message to Dad. With those pants nobody will take me for a boy."

Mother, a wonderful person who always entered into the spirit of adventure, capitulated. She walked me to the corner, but like an understanding mother, she let me board the car by myself. She did wave at me as the car started. She admitted later that she prayed for me until I returned home safely. "Good man," she said as she greeted me.

When we lived in Norwood, an independent small city surrounded by Cincinnati, a high official of the Cincinnati Reds National League baseball club, Frank Bancroft, was a near neighbor and a good friend of our family. He knew that we all were Reds fans and occasionally would supply us with free tickets to the games. Mother was as avid a fan as Dad, and many is the time when we sat in the stands, eating peanuts and popcorn and applauding our favorites when they won or groaning when they lost.

Mr. Bancroft, an outgoing and friendly man, had an attractive daughter, and the Reds players sometimes came to Spencer Avenue. Mr. Bancroft would invite all the kids along the street to come and meet the players. I had the opportunity of shaking hands with some of the most famous players of big league baseball in that era, including Ty Cobb and Christy Mathewson.

The 1910 census indicated that the population of the United States was 92 million—50 million on farms and rural areas, and 42 million as urban dwellers. The Irish had the highest literacy rate of immigrants, but Americans were not generally well educated. Less than half the population over the age of twenty-five had a high school diploma and only 4 percent had a college degree. It was the decade in which the Federal Income Tax was imposed, a tax which was promised never to exceed 10 percent. The great organist, doctor, and humanitarian, Albert Schweitzer, began his famous hospital work in Lambaréné, Africa. The Panama Canal, connecting the Atlantic and Pacific, was opened to international traffic. In 1914 President Wilson signed a joint resolution by Congress creating Mother's Day on the second Sunday in May.

Many things happened for the well-being of people in this second decade of the twentieth century. For one thing, the Cadillac car adopted Mr. Charles Kettering's electrical system for igniting an automobile engine, thereby doing away with the necessity of cranking a car to start it. It was called a self-starter. This one improvement in motor cars increased the number of women drivers, for most women before were fearful of cranking a car.

In 1911 songwriter Irving Berlin produced the famous "Alexander's Ragtime Band," and in 1912 the psychologist C. J. Jung introduced his theory of psychoanalysis. Woodrow Wilson, former governor of New Jersey, was elected president of the United States over the incumbent William Howard Taft, Republican, and former President Theodore Roosevelt, running as a progressive on the "Bull Moose" ticket, which had split off from the Republican party.

We had moved to Greenville, Ohio, where Father had become pastor of the Methodist church. This is a beautiful, small city close by the Indiana state line. I got a job representing the Cincinnati *Enquirer*, one of the most distinguished papers in Ohio. That is to say, I developed a paper route composed of customers who desired a newspaper of impeccable reliability. The *Enquirer* is a morning paper, and I had to meet a train at 5:30 A.M., get my papers off the train and hustle to deliver them all, and be at school by nine o'clock.

One morning I had a shock that I recall to this day. Opening my papers, I was riveted by a headline spread across the front page. In huge black letters the news of the greatest tragedy of the decade and, in fact, of several decades, leaped from the page: "Eighteen Hundred Lives Are Lost in Atlantic Ocean When Leviathan *Titanic* Plunges into the Depths: World-Famous Personages Are among the Dead."

The date was April 16, 1912.

Standing there reading the graphic story, I was never to forget the impact it made upon me, particularly the statement that as the greatest ship built up to that time went down on its maiden voyage, some of those in lifeboats could hear the ship's band on the sinking deck playing the old hymn "Nearer, My God, to Thee."

Years later I met a lady who survived that shipwreck. She was a young woman at the time and had been pulled out of the icy water by those in a lifeboat. Aghast, she and all in the lifeboat watched, terrified, as the great ship upended and slipped beneath the surface of the freezing sea. Then a sturdy seaman in charge of the lifeboat broke out of his stupefied reaction, as if he was coming out of a trance. He shouted, "Sing, damn you!" and he broke into the old hymn, "Jesus, Savior, pilot me over life's tempestuous sea." Those who didn't know the words joined in the tune, and as the sailors rowed away from that dying ship, all were singing. She said it helped them to cope with "the awful scene" they had just witnessed. They were rescued later that morning by the SS *Carpathia*.

A few years ago, more than seventy years after the *Titanic* disaster, I went back to Greenville and walked along Fourth Street, trying to pick out the house where we had lived. All the houses along the street looked somewhat different, due to architectural changes and the passage of time.

Finally one house seemed likely, and I rang the doorbell. A young man answered the ring. "Was this house ever the Methodist parsonage?"

"Why, yes, it was. The minister now lives—" and he started to give an address.

"No," I said, "I lived here once with my father and mother and brother."

"What's your name?" he asked.

"Norman Peale," I said, whereupon he turned and called to his wife, saying, "Please come and meet this man. He is the one whose name is carved in the attic." Then he said to me, "Would you like to see it?"

Surprised, I said I would.

They took me to the attic and sure enough, carved into a beam in deep, large block letters was my name and the date: "Norman Peale, Jan. 1, 1912." I have no recollection of having done that carving. Why does a young boy do a thing like that? I recall reading somewhere that in the ruins of ancient Rome a brick was found, marked "Romulus the slave." Now why did Romulus do that? Perhaps the desire to be remembered or just because people like to carve their names or initials someplace.

I then went up the block and across to where the old high school stood and where Lowell Thomas went to school, though before my time. (He was later my neighbor and close friend at Quaker Hill, Pawling, New York. I conducted his funeral in New York City in 1981.)

As I stood in front of that high school building, memories

crowded my mind. One incident was when several classmates and I painted the date of our class on the sidewalk—a gigantic "'16."

Next day in the school assembly, John Martz, the principal, who believed in honesty and expected honesty in students, asked, "Who painted the class numeral on the sidewalk? We are all honest in this school, and I expect whoever did it to confess now. You will be punished. But you are men enough to take it." A dead silence fell, and Mr. Martz waited.

Finally, I spoke up and said, "I did it, Mr. Martz." He did not ask the names of my coconspirators, for he wanted each one to "fess up," honestly, which they did, one by one. He made us wash off the numbers and that was hard going. Then he gave each of us a paddling. This was done in those days, and no one thought anything of it, except those who were paddled!

I asked an elderly passerby where I could find John Martz, who used to be principal of the high school. To my regret, I learned that he was deceased, but I was glad to know that Mrs. Martz was living. I went to see her, and we had a pleasant talk about old times. As I was leaving, she said, "Norman, John often used to say that he hated to give you a paddling that time. But he said it probably did you good." And maybe it did indeed.

On April 20, 1912, Bob and I were in a baseball game back of our house in a vacant lot. Bob had just hit a beautiful two-bagger and came into second base standing up, when our housekeeper, a middle-aged lady, came running, waving her hands at us. "You have a baby brother," she called in excitement. "He was born just about an hour ago. Your father called just now from Christ Hospital in Cincinnati."

Kids in a ball game are not likely to let a mere baby interfere, and play resumed. Bob came across home plate scoring a run for our side.

We decided to go to the "picture show" that evening to

celebrate the arrival of our new brother, Leonard Delaney Peale. But we were summoned from the theater to be told we must come at once, that the baby might die.

Arriving at Christ Hospital we tiptoed in, hand in hand, to see the baby, whose life was hanging in the balance. But in answer to prayer and good medical attention, Leonard survived to live a creative life. He was a very sincere and happy Christian, became a Methodist minister, and was loved in every church he served.

Later he became director of Outreach, one of the three departments of *Guideposts* magazine. In his retirement he and his wife, Josephine, lived in Venice, Florida, where Leonard served on the staff of Grace United Methodist Church. His radiant and happy spirit made him very popular in the church in Venice and in the community as well.

Leonard died suddenly on August 19, 1983, and the church erected a beautiful chapel in his memory called The Leonard Delaney Peale Memorial Chapel.

My father was transferred in 1913 to Bellefontaine, Ohio, where my graduation from high school was in the class of 1916. Then I entered Ohio Wesleyan University at Delaware, Ohio, and graduated in the class of 1920.

In 1912 an Ohio dentist, Zane Grey, gave up dental instruments and took a pen. With it he wrote *Riders of the Purple Sage*, which has become one of the immortal classics about the old West. Zane Grey is, in my opinion, one of the greatest masters of descriptions of nature. His books were best-sellers for years and are still selling. I have them all, together with those of a modern western writer, also of unparalleled genius, Louis L'Amour, recently deceased.

In 1912 a popular mail order company was inaugurated by L. L. Bean. Nearly eighty years later it's still going strong. On April 24, 1913, the Woolworth building in New York was lit up by President Wilson with the flick of a switch, as it was acclaimed the tallest building in the world. The Federal Reserve Board was created by an act of Congress on December 23, 1913. A Detroit newspaper on January 5, 1914, printed an unusual story about industrialist Henry Ford that electrified the nation. Ford's statement that the automobile would soon cause horses to disappear from American highways was proved true. And the automobile is credited with changing the business life of America, as well as effecting changes in social habits and even the morality of the country.

In the early part of the century dirt roads caused neighboring towns to be isolated, except those on the main line of a railroad or reachable by a branch line, of which there were many. With the advent of the motorcar, every town and village improved a short section of road at each end of the town called "the tar bound." It was a one-lane stretch of macadam roadway for about three miles. This was all a town had the finances to build. But gradually the states took over road building, which by the late 1950s resulted in the magnificent highway system of the nation.

These three miles of tar-bound roads were for a time about as far as a car would get before a tire would blow out or the machine develop engine trouble. Roads were deep in dust so that all motorists wore linen "dusters" similar to a rain coat, but longer, completely covering one's street clothes. A popular song of the time was "You'll Have to Get Out and Get Under." Cars broke down much of the time, and the driver "got out and got under" to see where the trouble was. The automobile may be credited with an historic addition to the economy by stimulating many new businesses such as tire production, the petroleum industry, all highway services, garages, motels, and others.

Americans became irate over the sinking of the SS *Lusitania* on May 7, 1915, drowning 1200 passengers, of whom 128 were American citizens. Commuters at the Third Avenue elevated Hanover Station stood solemnly when they heard the news and spontaneously sang, "In the Sweet By and By." Former President Theodore Roosevelt furiously described the vessel's sinking as "an act of piracy and international murder." The incident poisoned relations between the United States and Germany.

It was a time of great anxiety. On orders from the German Kaiser, all the might of German military force had been hurled against Belgium and France in 1914. The First World War was on in Europe. But life went on about as usual in the U.S. We were, for the time being, kept out of war. Nevertheless, Americans were nervous about the situation.

Finally, after many German violations of our neutrality, an emotional session of Congress on April 6, 1917, produced a declaration of war against the German Empire. President Wilson, who owed his re-election to his policy of keeping us out of war, sadly asked the Congress to declare war, "not in search of conquest, but to ensure universal right."

Former President Theodore Roosevelt was in favor of America's entrance into the war. He was extremely patriotic and offered his services as a military leader, an offer that was declined because of his age.

I was an avid follower of Theodore Roosevelt. He was a political cyclone and perhaps the first great progressive in the modern sense. He came of a New York society family and was a cum laude scholar at Harvard. He was far from the log cabin tradition, yet he was idolized by people of every level and every type of American. It was his incredible energy and enthusiasm, his interest in just about everything, his spirit of adventure, his love of people, and his flaming patriotism that endeared him to everyone.

He lived life to the hilt. As a romantic political leader he was personally quite irresistible, whether or not one went along with all his ideas. One thing is sure, he was the political idol of my youth, and the young people of that era were generally captivated by TR. I met him only once. John Joseph, a classmate at Ohio Wesleyan in Delaware, Ohio, heard that Roosevelt was to speak in Columbus. We went to hear him as he spoke on the lawn of the state capitol.

His youngest son, Quentin, had recently lost his life, shot down over Germany on a flying mission. He was buried by enemy aviators in a German village with full military honors. Ex-President Roosevelt took it hard. He said, "We raised our boys to be eagles and did not expect them to act like sparrows." But we thought the sorrow had aged him. The old fire just wasn't in his speech that day. And yet, after the speech, with the crowds pressing him, he took time for two young men. He spent several minutes saying to us, "Live life with enthusiasm. Be good Americans. Help people to live a better, more successful life. Never lose the true youthful spirit." He died of an embolism not long after that.

John Joseph and I went to the balcony of Gray Chapel on the campus to read the *Ohio State Journal*'s account of his passing. A cartoon pictured TR on a prancing horse, and the caption read, "Into eternity rides Theodore Roosevelt, dreamer of dreams." We wept and recalled that day in Columbus when he was not too busy to talk to two young men.

Ohio Wesleyan, in the period I was a student there, 1916–1920, was governed by rules and regulations that by today's standards would probably be considered old-fashioned. For example, if you took a date out for dinner or an entertainment, you had to get her back within Monnet Hall, the women's dormitory, by 9:00 P.M., or else.

I fell afoul of this rule once. Another Phi Gamma Delta

fraternity brother and I took two girls to Bun's Restaurant for dinner and then to some entertainment. It was nine-thirty or ten when we arrived back at Monnet Hall. What were we to do? We knew the location of a ladder and quietly put it up against a wall where there was an unlocked window. My fellow conspirator got his girl through the window and was undetected in the process. Unfortunately, mounting the ladder to survey the situation, I found myself looking squarely into the face of the dean of women. "So, Norman," she said rather icily, "you seem quite expert in climbing ladders. Tell your lady friend to come to the front door, where I shall meet her for a little talk. And as for you, see me in my office in Administration tomorrow morning."

The next day I showed up as directed. The dean of women, who sat across from me, was destined to become a close friend of both Ruth and me many years later in New York, where I would call her "Kathryn," but this day I was looking at a no-nonsense administrator. "We are trying to do the best we can for you while here, Norman. Don't let this occur again." It didn't, and in later years Kathryn Phillips, as she was known then, opined at a dinner party, looking at me, "Discipline is good for the young," to which I answered, "Amen."

At the Phi Gamma Delta fraternity house, called "Fairbanks Lodge" in honor of the vice president of the United States, Hon. Charles W. Fairbanks, himself a member of the fraternity, the boys were quartered two to a room, with a double-decker bed. An upper classman had a freshman as roommate. I was quartered with the president of the chapter, Cecil J. Wilkinson, called "Scoop," he being editor of the college paper, *The Transcript*. Scoop, of course, occupied the lower bunk and I, as a lowly freshman, climbed to the upper. After opening the windows on bitterly cold nights, I would snuggle down under the covers.

Often the senior would say in a stern voice, "Freshman Peale, I have a desire to gaze on the face of Nell once more before Morpheus puts me to sleep. Get up and turn on the light that I may see my beloved's face." He was engaged to Nell Herbert, a lovely girl. I would have to crawl down into that frigid room and turn on the light, while Scoop took plenty of time looking at Nell's picture. But I loved both of them just the same and was always proud that I had the privilege of rooming with a boy who became a truly great man in later years, creatively working with youth.

When in my senior year I became president of the chapter, my younger brother Bob was my freshman roommate. One Saturday night some of the boys were having a beer party in the library downstairs. I had gone down to see them, when Bob, in bathrobe, suddenly appeared at the top of the stairs. He called, "Norman, come up here at once."

"Be quiet, freshman," I said, whereupon he declared, "I'll come down and knock your block off if you don't come up here at once."

So I came up. "What are you so worked up about?" I asked.

"I don't want you at a beer party," he said.

"I wasn't drinking," I protested.

"No matter," said he. "I know that, but I don't want you even around it." Bob watched over his older brother all his life. He became a physician and surgeon, and a good one, too.

One of the most important, life-determining experiences I ever had occurred when I was a sophomore at Ohio Wesleyan. In fact, it was a momentous happening that turned my life around. I had a class in economics with Professor Ben Arneson. I was very shy and bashful, with my recurring problem with low self-esteem, and always slipped to a back and inconspicuous seat in the classroom where I hoped I would be unnoticed. But the professor called upon me to explain a point in that day's lesson. Despite my inferiority feelings, I was a hard worker and was up on the material. But my shyness made me tongue-tied and embarrassed when called upon to speak in public. I grew red in the face, nervously shifted from one foot to the other, and explained the point ineffectively. I sat down, overcome by confusion and well aware that I had made an exhibition of myself.

When the class was about to adjourn, Professor Arneson made a few announcements, then said, "Peale, please remain after class. I want to talk with you." After the others had gone, he beckoned me to a chair opposite his desk. He was bouncing a round eraser up and down, meanwhile looking at me with what I thought was a piercing gaze.

"What's the matter with you, son? You have mastered the material in this course and probably will get a good grade. But you are so horribly embarrassed and self-effacing."

"Well, Professor, I guess I have a big inferiority complex."

"Would you like to get over it and become a normal person?"

I nodded. "But how?"

"You might try the way I overcame my inferiority complex." Startled, I looked at this big, rugged man. "Professor, you had the same trouble I have?" He nodded. "But what did you do to get over it?"

He sat looking at me kindly. "I simply asked God to help me, and believed that He would. He did. Get going, Peale, and God bless you."

I stumbled out and down the steps in front of the building. I stopped on the fourth step from the bottom and said a prayer. "Dear Lord, You can take a drunk and make him sober, a thief and make him honest. Can't you also take a mixed-up boy like me and make me normal? I believe You will. Thank You. Amen."

I stood there expecting a miracle. And a miracle did happen, but over a period of time. Gradually I made much progress in my struggle with painful self-consciousness. I am still shy, but the difference is I can now control it.

As sophomores some of us concocted a money-making scheme, for we were always broke. We would sell "campus tickets" to unsuspecting and green freshman for one dollar. And that was real money at that time. We amassed a couple of hundred dollars before the administration, unimpressed with our creativity, notified the freshmen that admission to the campus was free to all.

The war came to the campus in the form of the Student Army Training Corp. The SATC was described as being a pretraining for officers' training school, to which presumably we would be transferred as soon as we were adjudged suitable material for officers in the army. Captain Loman, a highly competent but tough regular army officer, became our commander.

We were all ordered to move out of our comfortable quarters in fraternity houses and dormitories and were installed in barracks like troops. There we lived under strict army rules. We had to go to bed in our army cots when taps was sounded, and we were awakened by a bugle's harsh notes at early morning reveille.

I happened to be appointed first lieutenant of our company and an upper classman was made student captain. We were issued regular uniforms and were instructed to wear them at all times. We lived by the regular rules of the military.

Our company was quartered in the YMCA building, which was taken over as a barracks for our company; and we were marched to Edwards Gymnasium on the campus, perhaps a mile away, for meals with the entire student troop. We continued going to classes.

One morning the company filed out of the barracks and

lined up to be marched to breakfast at the gym. Suddenly the captain barked an order, "Lieutenant Peale, form the company and proceed to chow." My own military training had been rather sketchy, and I had only a foggy idea of how to proceed. The boys were aware of this, and, while they were all my friends, they were still boys and not averse to making it tough for their first lieutenant.

But I saluted smartly and said, "Yes sir." I then rasped out, as tough as I could make it, the command, "Company, attention! Fall in! Dress right! Forward march!" We were quickly off the parade ground, and I had speedily to determine whether to order the company to turn right or left. While I was considering, we came to the street corner where George Buchman's Saloon was located. Now the rules of the university, if not the army, strictly forbade entering a saloon. But the column continued to march straight ahead, despite my shouts, and plunged laughing into the saloon. "Hey, you guys, come out of there!" I shouted desperately.

Not viewing this as a properly expressed military order, they milled about laughing and slapping each other's shoulders and having a riotous and hilarious time. Finally, taking pity on their commander, they formed company and marched docilely to breakfast. This may explain why I never became a general!

A detachment, in which I was included, was ordered to proceed to officers' training, but the Armistice came on November 11, 1918, and the order was countermanded. Presently came the order for mustering out of the student army, and the university went on a peacetime schedule.

An American army newspaper article from Compiègne, France, for that day read,

> *The Great War is over. The Germans signed an armistice agreement at 5:00 A.M. here and it went into effect at eleven*

o'clock. President Wilson made it official when he informed both houses of Congress today that "the war thus comes to an end."

The cost of the war was unbelievable. The Allies mobilized more than 42 million men, and 5 million of them were killed, including 116,516 Americans. There were 21 million wounded combatants in all. The Central Powers mobilized 23 million men, of whom at least 3.4 million were killed.

War expenditure figures differ widely, but the best guess for the Allied effort is $30 trillion; America contributed $32 billion to that total. And still, the figures do not tell the saddest story of all—the obliteration of a whole generation of young men on the Western Front. Who knows how many fine poems and scientific discoveries will never belong to humanity because the poet and scientist were destroyed in the bloom of their youth.

The young army soldier Joyce Kilmer, who was killed at the front, was one such talented man who gave us the much loved poem "Trees."

I think that I shall never see
A poem lovely as a tree.
A tree whose hungry mouth is pressed
Against the earth's sweet flowing breast;
A tree that looks at God all day,
And lifts her leafy arms to pray;
A tree that may in Summer wear
A nest of robins in her hair;
Upon whose bosom snow has lain;
Who intimately lives with rain.
Poems are made by fools like me,
But only God can make a tree.

As if the war wasn't horrible enough, in the fall of 1918 the Spanish flu struck America with dire effect. One quarter of the American population was infected and hundreds died in the worst flu epidemic in history.

In December 1918, President Wilson went to the Paris Peace Conference and triumphantly returned on February 14, 1919, with the League of Nations project. Due to senatorial opposition to the League, he took it to the people in a nation-wide speaking tour, which resulted in broken health for the president. The League of Nations was finally rejected by the Senate by a vote of 53 to 38.

I once had a brief conversation with President Wilson during his speaking tour in behalf of the League of Nations. A classmate and I were walking on Broad Street in Columbus on the north side of the State House, as the state capitol building is called. Suddenly Phil said, "Do you know who is approaching?"

"Who?" I asked.

"No less than the president of the United States."

I started to say, "Don't kid me," when I recognized the figure of Woodrow Wilson, walking with a cane and followed by two stocky men, presumably bodyguards. Phil, who was quite out going and not as reticent as I, doffed his hat. We all wore hats in those days. He said very respectfully, "Good morning, Mr. President."

Mr. Wilson smiled and stopped and extended his hand. "Good morning, men," he responded. I thought it noteworthy that he did not call us "boys" but "men." It was the professor in him, I suppose, for he had been a professor and later the president of Princeton University.

He inquired if we were Ohio State students, and when we told him we were Ohio Wesleyan, he said, "Good, that is a fine school founded by godly people long ago. I believe in the partnership of religion and education. They belong together, God being the first cause of all life." Those are not guaranteed to be his exact words, but the general idea was as stated. He talked with us for several minutes, then said, "Good-bye," adding, "I wish all good things for you in life," with which he continued his walk around the capitol.

We remarked to each other that the president was more outgoing than the press made him out to be. I read in that evening's newspaper that a truck driver had leaned out of his truck and called to the president, "Hello there, Woody. How you doin'?"

Woodrow Wilson, usually portrayed as being scholarly and aloof, waved back with a grin, saying, "Fine and I hope you are, too." Later he commented, "First time anyone called me 'Woody.' Perhaps I'm making progress."

CHAPTER 3

The Roaring Twenties

A T 12:01 A.M. on January 16, 1920, the Eighteenth Amendment to the Constitution of the United States went into effect. It was the beginning of the Prohibition era. Since my grandmother, Laura Peale, had been a founder of the WCTU (Women's Christian Temperance Union), and my father had been active in the movement to make Ohio "dry," several of us students at Ohio Wesleyan went to Columbus to see the festivities—or obsequies, depending upon how one felt about it.

At the corner of Broad and High Streets stood a big saloon run by an obviously law-respecting man. Promptly at midnight he began rolling wooden kegs of whiskey to the curb; unplugging them, he let the contents spill into the gutter. This continued until his stock, now illicit, had all been dumped into the street, running like rainwater toward the nearby river. One wag, noting the direction of this flow, began singing the old hymn "Shall We Gather at the River?"

The crowd expressed mixed reactions, some showing resentment, some thanking God for "this great day." Billy Sunday had left big league baseball to become the great evangelist of the era. When Prohibition came that January 16, he held a "funeral" service in Norfolk, Virginia, attended by thousands, in which he "buried John Barleycorn," as liquor was sometimes called. Ever a showman, he arranged for a special train carrying a simulated coffin of John Barleycorn. Sunday bade Barleycorn farewell, saying, "Good-bye, John. You were God's worst enemy; you were hell's best friend."

Billy was a preacher of rare power. I heard him often. And he achieved spectacular results. Once in a New York revival he is said to have converted 100,000 people to the Christian faith. I knew many of these converts who kept the faith all their lives, while some fell away.

Writers of books, magazines, and newspapers called the third decade of the twentieth century "The Roaring Twenties." It was the era of a changing America: the flapper girl, Teapot Dome, the Ku Klux Klan, Lindbergh flying the Atlantic, the beginning of the Great Depression, the era of "fads, flappers, and fashion."

Ivy League dropout F. Scott Fitzgerald, in his book *This Side of Paradise*, came out with this historic assertion, "Here was a new generation grown up to find all gods dead, all wars fought, all faiths in men shaken." And Sinclair Lewis, with his widely read book *Main Street*, was among the first of a long series of writers who chipped away at the value system that had built the country. It was a time of pleasure-seeking, doubt, and greed.

As the Roaring Twenties began, there was intense interest in the presidential election of 1920. Who would be nominated? The Ohio State Republican organization was for native son Senator Warren G. Harding, who had never done anything of particular note but was "one of the boys." We who were the graduates in 1920 had more idealistic views and were for General Leonard Wood. He was a progressive and vied with Senator Hiram Johnson of California for the nomination. Harding had little support other than from the Ohio organization. The Wood campaign was well financed and seemed to be gathering momentum as our senior year drew to a close. Wood's organization made a strong effort for the Wood campaign to conduct polls in the colleges of the state, which would come out in favor of General Wood to indicate that educated people were for him.

I had a letter from Wood headquarters in Columbus, asking to "consult" me about carrying the Ohio Wesleyan student body for their candidate. Would I come down to the capital at a certain time to talk it over? I took this up with John Joseph, a classmate who had political leanings toward General Wood, and he readily agreed to accompany me.

Wood headquarters were two rooms in the old Hotel Neal House, which stood on High Street directly opposite the State House. In charge was a fat man who extended his pudgy hand with a genial "Welcome, gentlemen," a greeting that went over big with us.

"We understand you gentlemen are very influential in the educational world, and we think that a vote in favor of our great intellectual candidate, General Wood, will help greatly in assuring him the Republican nomination at Chicago in June. We want to give you railroad tickets to Chicago for the convention."

When we replied that our commencement was at the same time, he expressed deep regret. "Well, then you will be working on the home front." He took out of a drawer a stack of bills that John later inelegantly said "would choke a cow." He asked, "How much do you want in order to carry Ohio Wesleyan?"

I started to say we would do it for nothing, but before I could get the words fully out, John kicked me under the table. He told the man that he figured we would need about $200 if he could spare it. Accordingly, the fellow peeled off five twenty-dollar bills and handed them to John, then counted out another five twenties, which he gave to me. "There's more where they came from, if needed," he remarked.

He then told us that the candidate was to appear in person in Memorial Hall on a certain date. "And we want you gentlemen to sit with the general on the stage that night. See you then. And get us a big majority." We used up most of the money in printing costs and in paying for ads in local papers. The poll of the student body resulted in a sizeable majority for General Wood.

The night of the big Wood rally in Memorial Hall, we were on hand early in the room off the stage where the platform party was assembled. John and I had seats in the back row, but we bowed to the packed house, which was tumultuously applauding General Wood. Well, the General couldn't garner enough votes at the convention, and Harding was selected by the party bosses to break a deadlock. This was my only experience in politics, and it was somewhat enlightening on how things work. I have since eschewed politics, and I think a minister should never take a partisan stand unless some moral issue is involved. He is bound to hurt his spiritual ministry if he is considered "political."

Probably the big story of the decade was that women, who comprised half of the population, were finally given the right to vote by the ratification of the Nineteenth Amendment to the Constitution. This was certified by Bainbridge Colby, Secretary of State, on August 26, 1920.

I shall always be proud that my bright and intelligent mother, heretofore denied the citizen's basic right of suffrage, and I went together, each for the first time, to the polling place to vote for the president on November 2, 1920. On my previous birthday I had become twenty-one years of age, which was then the voting age.

The candidates for president that year were both from Ohio,

and we knew them personally. The Democratic candidate was former Governor James M. Cox, publisher of the Dayton *Daily News*. The Republican candidate was Senator Warren G. Harding of Marion, Ohio, the man who had defeated my candidate, Leonard Wood, for the nomination. The Republican candidate for vice president was Calvin Coolidge, governor of Massachusetts. The Democratic vice presidential candidate was Franklin D. Roosevelt.

Harding and Coolidge won by a landslide despite Harding's selection, as one pundit described it, "in a smoke-filled room" at the Chicago Republican Convention after a deadlock. Both of the vice presidential candidates later became president. Mother and I lined up together at the polls. I insisted on her preceding me. "Ladies first," I said.

"Humph," she replied, "took men a long time to become gallant." Pointing to the town drunk, she added, "And he has been voting for years."

When we had both voted, I said, "Whom did you vote for?"

She drew herself up in mock dignity. "That is a private matter." Then her curiosity got the best of her, and she remarked, "And I suppose you voted for that old no-good Warren Harding, just like your father. You voted Republican because the Peale men have always followed along like sheep and been Republicans. As for me, I'm a thoughtful, nonpartisan independent."

"Bet you voted for Cox, the Democratic candidate."

"Well, suppose I did. I arrived at that opinion by objective thought and not by tradition."

"Mama," I said, "with all due respect for your independent, thoughtful voting, I seem to recall that your father and grandfather were both dyed-in-the-wool Democrats."

As for myself, I didn't vote for Harding with any enthusiasm and would have been glad if Cox had won.

Anyhow, Mother and I walked together from the polls, loving and respecting each other as mother and son, despite politics.

KDKA in Pittsburgh has usually been accepted as national radio broadcasting's first licensed commercial station. It started on that election day, November 2, 1920, with a good deal of static and crackle. The station announced election returns, sponsored by Westinghouse, but fewer than a thousand receivers were tuned to the broadcast. However, even this small beginning spurred national interest in radio broadcasting.

My research indicates that a station on the West Coast, at San Jose, California, has a prior claim as the first station. It was KQW, now called KCBS, and it was experimentally built and developed by Charles D. Harrold some eleven years earlier, in 1909. It broadcast music (played on a Victrola near the microphone) and news, read from the newspaper by Harrold.

In June I had graduated from college in the class of 1920. Father, congratulating me, said, "Now, let your light shine."

Mother said, "God wants you to serve Him. We have put you through college to qualify you to do great things. God bless you, Son."

I returned home to Findlay, Ohio, and went to work as a reporter for the Findlay *Morning Republican.* Life was getting more and more exciting for a young person just graduated from college and looking to the future.

A newspaper clipping of 1920 succinctly gives one version of what was happening in America at the time.

> *What's cooking tonight—meat and potatoes—now Americans are going for new brand names featuring Underwood sardines, Maxwell House Coffee (it's good to the last drop— Teddy Roosevelt once said so), Kellogg's All-Bran cereal, Camp Fire marshmallows, Good Humor ice cream and Baby Ruth bars (named for the daughter of former President*

*Grover Cleveland). Everything is easier nowadays. The ice
chest is out, the Frigidaire is in; silk stockings are out, rayon
hosiery is in. It's tough deciding on an automobile—a Ford,
Cadillac, Franklin, Chalmers-Franklin, Packard, or Pierce-
Arrow.*

It was a changing America in the twenties. The dollar was
still strong. You could get a good square meal for a dollar and
a half, and even in New York you could have a good lunch for
a half dollar.

Some not-so-nice things were happening in our still religious, ethical, and moral country. Fans were shocked in 1920
by charges that the Chicago White Sox had deliberately lost
the 1919 World Series with the Cincinnati Reds in the worst
scandal in the history of the American game. Judge Kenesaw
Mountain Landis became the first commissioner for baseball
in 1920, and in an effort to restore the tarnished image of the
sport, he banned some of the most famous players accused of
conspiring to throw the 1919 World Series in exchange for
money from gambling interests. Judge Landis succeeded in
clearing the reputation of the game as an honest sport.

I remember this scandal very well indeed, for I had always
been an avid fan of the Reds, and all Reds fans had been excited
when Cincinnati won the National League Pennant in 1919.
Our joy was turned into sorrow when it was revealed that the
White Sox players sold out for money.

While all these things were going on in the Roaring Twenties, I was learning my job as a reporter on the *Morning
Republican,* one of the best small-city dailies in the country. I
worked for Mr. I. N. Heminger, and my first job was to make
the rounds of undertaking or funeral establishments to see who
had died and then to write obituary notices for publication. I
must have done this fairly well, for one of the city's leading
citizens is reputed to have remarked that "it maybe would be

worth dying to have one of Peale's affecting obituary stories written about one." But then he added, "If you were deceased, of course, you couldn't read it."

My editor, the late Anson Hardman, assigned me to report the deliberations of the city council. I sat at the press table with the reporter from the *Courier*, an afternoon paper. He was Irwin Geffs, a kindly man much older than I and one of the best writers I have ever encountered. He gave me valuable advice and was a good friend to a young reporter.

As I think back on the first three decades of the nine I have lived, the invaluable influence of my parents was impressive. And parental influence on most American youth was also motivating, strong, and positive. In the early years of the 1900s we called our mother "Mama" and our father "Papa." Then later, probably in the twenties, it became popular to call father "Dad" and mother "Mom." But somehow I usually called them Father and Mother. I never referred to my father as the "old man." I was brought up to respect my parents highly. They did everything to help their boys develop into good men.

Mother was a remarkable woman. Perhaps she was born before her time. Had she lived in this present era when women are taking leadership roles, she would, with her natural talents, have been outstanding. As it was, even in the early part of the century, she was a gifted and popular public speaker. In Findlay she was the first woman elected to the board of education. She was a leader of the Foreign Missionary Society of the Methodist church and traveled over much of Asia in this activity. On her gravestone it states "world missionary leader." She had perfect concentration and a photographic mind: she could read a page of copy and repeat it almost verbatim. Her grasp and knowledge of English and American literature was phenomenal. And above all, she was a beautiful, in-depth Christian lady.

The twenties was the era of the flapper and the Charleston dance. But while women were experiencing more freedom, and some abused that freedom, the general moral standards were essentially unchanged. The practice of unmarried people living together had not yet come about. The flapper wore her skirts just above the knees and the magazine *Vanity Fair* said she "wears rouge and lipstick and may drink in public."

During my college days, except for a daring few, young women wore their skirts at ankle length, and men wore suits, ties, and hats. The hatless style was of much later vintage. Lowell Thomas, the famous radio commentator, traveler, and writer, told me once, when he saw me on the street without a hat, "A man isn't dressed without a hat." He always wore one, right up until his death in 1981.

I received an offer to join the staff of the *Detroit Journal* in 1921, and, thinking it might be a valuable opportunity, I accepted. It was with great regret that I left the Heminger family, but I was to enjoy a lifetime friendship with them.

The editor of the *Detroit Journal* at this time was Grove Patterson, a very prominent publisher and man of great wisdom. The first day I worked for him he asked, "As a reporter, to whom will you write? Let's say a learned scholar at the university, or a person with only grammar school education, perhaps a day laborer?"

"I will write to the man of grammar school education, the day laborer, then both readers will understand."

Then he put what I thought was a dot on a sheet of paper. "What is that?" he asked.

"A dot," I replied.

"It is a period, the greatest of all literary devices. Its function is to stop a sentence. Never write past a period. Use simple, fast-paced sentences of short simple words. Create description in simple language forms." When later I left the paper to study for the ministry, he said, "Use the same principles of writing in your sermons and speeches and people will listen to you."

Beginning in 1921 the American economy surged in a period of unparalleled prosperity that lasted for about eight years. Industrial expansion and creation of wealth marked the decade. The income of American citizens increased. Indeed, the United States economy became the wonder of the world. A consideration of the prosperity of the twenties lends seriousness to the statement of an American businessman, Joseph Dunkle, who has become a successful entrepreneur in Japan: "America once electrified the world by creating wealth; now in the decade of the eighties it is churning wealth by mergers and through buying and selling companies that once created prosperity."

I was an enthusiastic and energetic young fellow in my early twenties and enjoyed being a reporter on a newspaper in Detroit, a city fast becoming the motorcar capital of the world. I thought the newsroom on Jefferson Avenue was just about the center of everything.

Early in my work on the paper I was assigned to cover a trial across the river in Windsor, Ontario. The details of this trial, which were very interesting at the time, have faded with the years, except that I well recall the opposing attorneys. Tobacco chewing was much in vogue at the time, and these two attorneys seemed to be copious chewers of the weed.

As these attorneys walked to and fro during arguments, I, together with the spectators, the jury, and perhaps even the judge, became fascinated in speculating which of them could expectorate the greatest distance and accurately hit the shining brass spittoon, causing it to ring like a bell. I remember that this judicial spitting contest found a place in my reports of the trial and got by the editorial pencil of my hard-boiled editor. In fact, he averred later, "Quite a classic story, Peale, particularly that spitting bit."

I had many fascinating experiences in my work as a reporter, and life was very exciting. But perhaps the most meaningful experience of all, judged by its personal impact, happened one night. The fire alarm, which was registered in our newsroom by telephone, rang out that night, and the city editor said, "Peale, you cover this one." The fire was in a six-floor building, and a big crowd had gathered.

I pushed through the crowd to the fire line, showed my reporter's pass, and edged up front. I was informed that the stairways were aflame and the only elevator was also cut off.

There in an open window on the sixth floor was a little girl, who appeared to be eleven or twelve years of age, all alone and terrified. Someone had shoved an eight-foot plank across from an adjacent building, upon which firemen were sprinkling water to keep it from catching fire. This plank was about a foot wide. People were shouting to the little girl to crawl across. She would get on the plank and start, but then she would look down and draw back in obvious terror.

During a momentary hush I cried out, "Honey, do you believe in God?" She nodded. "Do you believe God is up there with you waiting to help you cross that plank?" Again she nodded. "He is there, for He said, 'I will be with you always.' Now don't look down. Look straight ahead and think about God."

She started and got well out on the plank, then seemed to hesitate. I called out again, "Don't look down, honey, just look straight ahead. God is with you and will see you all the way to that building. I am praying for you. All these people are praying for you. We love you. God loves you." With this encouragement she crawled to safety. Eager hands reached for her. The crowd, many with tears in their eyes, cheered. A burly police sergeant turned to me and said, "Good job, son. You sound like a preacher."

"I'm no preacher," I replied.

"The hell you're not!" he said.

I escaped from the crowd and walked for blocks. I was shaken to my depths. Back at my room I telephoned home. Dad answered, and I knew I had wakened him. I told him what had happened, then Mother took the telephone and I repeated the story. "I believe God is calling you to be a preacher," she said. "Your father and I are proud that He saved that little girl through you. Perhaps He wants you to save many."

But I continued with the reporter's job, all the time saying, "I don't know," to what had become an insistent call to become a preacher and pastor. Finally, I knew I had to come to a decision. It was hard, for I wanted to be a newspaper man. But finally I asked to see Mr. Patterson, my editor, and told him I had decided to be a minister. He was himself a great Christian, and he understood me. "Well, Norman, I congratulate you. You will hereafter still be a reporter telling the good news of the gospel." I was deeply moved. In order to save the interview from becoming tearful he said, "If you ever find that you don't like preaching or don't do very well at it, let me know. Your old job will always be waiting for you."

Many years later, sitting in the pulpit of a church on New York's Fifth Avenue, I spotted Patterson in the congregation. Perhaps I wanted my old editor to believe that his erstwhile reporter was not too bad in this new role, so I endeavored to preach my best. Later I was greeting people at the front of the church when I saw Grove Patterson approaching in the line. I guess that I expected a word of approval, but instead, with a rather dour look he said, "Well, Norman, your old job is still waiting for you." He was an inspiring, lifelong friend, and I revere his memory.

While still a reporter, I met President and Mrs. Warren G. Harding on a train in Ohio. They were seated in the parlor car, and people were going up to shake hands with them. Mr. Harding was friendly and affable, so finally I approached and said, "Mr. President, I'm a young fellow who is a newspaper reporter, and I know you are a publisher." (He published the Marion, Ohio, *Star*.) "What advice would you give a young reporter?"

He considered the question a long minute, then said, "Always have respect for the facts. Write interestingly and with human interest, using simple language." He was most gracious to me and to the others who spoke to him.

Only a year later, President Harding made a transcontinental speaking trip and was resting in the St. Francis Hotel in San Francisco. It was August 2, 1923, and Mrs. Harding was reading to him a favorable article on his presidency titled "Calm Review of a Calm Man." As she read, the president quietly breathed his last.

At that time I was a theological student at Boston University, living in Louisburg Square on Beacon Hill and taking a summer course. I went to breakfast at the New England Kitchen restaurant on nearby Charles Street on the morning of August 3, 1923, picked up my usual *Boston Herald*, and read of the death of President Harding. It also told the story of the swearing-in, the night before, of Vice President Calvin Coolidge as president by his father, a local justice of the peace, at the Coolidge farm in Vermont. It took place in typical American style of the time: by coal oil lamplight.

Calvin Coolidge as president achieved great popularity. He was known as "Silent Cal" because of his sparing speech. He is reported as saying, "I think the country wants a solemn president, and I think I'll go along with them." Many stories relate to his brevity with words, and one of the best was of the time he went to church alone. After he returned to the White House, at Sunday dinner Mrs. Coolidge asked, "What did the preacher preach about today?"

"Sin," replied Coolidge.

"And what did he say about sin?" persisted Mrs. Coolidge.

The president replied, "He was against it."

President Coolidge insisted that all who were guilty in the Teapot Dome scandal be fully prosecuted. It had to do with the misappropriation of federal lands and oil reserves in Wyoming. Secretary of the Interior Albert B. Fall was indicted, and two major oil company executives, Harry Sinclair and Edward L. Doheny, were accused of bribery and conspiracy.

President Coolidge, who inherited this government scandal, was insistent that all who were proven guilty be brought to justice. In a blistering comment to his secretary of commerce, Herbert Hoover, the president said, "There are only three purgatories to which people can be assigned: to be damned by one's fellows; to be damned by the courts; to be damned in the next world. I want these men to get all three without probation."

I had the pleasure of meeting this thoroughly honest man and president several times. One time was when my classmate, longtime friend and fellow Phi Gamma Delta brother, Webster D. Melcher, and I were together in Washington. I suggested to Webster that we call on my congressman from Ohio, the Honorable Clint Cole.

Mr. Cole asked us if we would like to meet the president, who was in the habit of holding a reception on Wednesdays at noon, to which members of Congress could bring constituents. Clint Cole said in his back-home manner, "Norman, you have Ohio mud on your shoes, and even if Webster here has Pennsylvania mud on his shoes, I will take you both in to meet Cal."

When the receiving line reached the president, with the audacity of youth I gave him the college Phi Gamma Delta fraternity grip, since I knew that Mr. Coolidge was also a member. He recognized the grip and returned it with a grin and said, "I belong to the Amherst chapter."

"I know that, Mr. President," I replied. That was the total conversation.

At a later time I had a few more words with Calvin Coolidge when he spoke in the old North Church in Boston, from which Paul Revere saw the lanterns that sped him on his famous midnight ride.

In 1924 I went to Brooklyn, New York, to become assistant minister of St. Marks Methodist Church on Ocean Avenue. But my principal duty was to build a church on King's Highway at 37th Street, which we named the King's Highway Methodist Church. I was pastor of this new church for three years, by which time it had about a thousand members and was one of the most active churches in Brooklyn.

While living in Brooklyn I met Frank Goodman, director of radio for the National Council of Churches, and he became one of my best friends. Frank lived just around the corner from King's Highway Church. Mrs. Goodman often invited me to dinner in their home. Frank would insist that I watch myself speak before a full-length mirror, with the explanation that I "had the makings of a good speaker but needed a little training." Later he made a place for my program "The Art of Living" on NBC. It went on every Saturday night for some thirty years.

In the spring of 1927 I was appointed by Bishop Adna Wright Leonard to be pastor of the University Avenue Methodist Church in Syracuse, New York. In May I drove to Syracuse, the same day that Charles Lindbergh made his epic flight across the Atlantic to Paris in a little plane called the *Spirit of St. Louis*.

Lindbergh, a shy midwesterner, was twenty-five years old when he made this solo, nonstop, historic flight. He landed in the French capital after a flight of thirty-three hours, a distance of thirty-six hundred miles.

Overloaded with gasoline, his plane took off "like a drunken seagull," barely clearing the trees at the end of the runway at Roosevelt Field on Long Island. But the flight was a go, and he flew along the coast, turning out over the Atlantic at St. John's, Newfoundland. From there Lindbergh flew by dead reckoning, often descending to ten feet above the sea, sometimes ascending to ten thousand feet. He occasionally took a bite of homemade sandwiches he had brought along.

Off Ireland, to be sure of directions, he came down to where fishermen were at work in their boats, and he shouted, "Which way is Paris?" He landed there at 10:24 P.M. to receive a tumultuous welcome from a vast throng. He became one of the great men of history.

At a later time, when living in New York City, I became acquainted with Colonel and Mrs. Lindbergh. They were dignified, private people, despite Colonel Lindbergh's being one of our most popular and revered figures, and Mrs. Lindbergh one of the most highly respected authors of the period. Her book *Listen! The Wind* was, I thought, particularly charming. I always felt the Lindberghs represented American culture at its best.

The transatlantic flight of Colonel Lindbergh was one of the great events in aviation history. It thrilled the world and was the forerunner of the great air transport network we have today.

In the 1920s it was a great time, and a sad time, in the world of sports. Just before the decade of the twenties, on July 4, 1919, in Toledo, the huge 250-pound heavyweight boxing champion Jess Willard, who had contemptuously belittled Jack Dempsey as "little Jack," was battered into defeat in three rounds by "little" Jack. Willard was unable to answer the bell for the fourth round. Dempsey, too, was exhausted but on his feet.

Negroes (as blacks or African-Americans were then called) organized the National Negro Baseball League early in 1920 with eight clubs. It is interesting to note that late in the 1800s some black players were included on all-white teams, but by 1900 they were excluded. In 1906 a league was formed of four black teams and two white teams. However, this league lasted for only one season. It remained for Jackie Robinson and Branch Rickey to permanently break the color barrier for athletes later, in 1947.

Another baseball item of 1920 was the purchase by the New York Yankees of the great homerun-hitter Babe Ruth. He hit fifty-four home runs in the 1920 season. And think of it: Babe Ruth earned only $20,000 salary, a bit different from the huge salaries paid to baseball players in the 1990s, even when one allows for the great inflation rate.

In 1925 a basketball league was formed. It comprised nine successful professional teams and was called the American Basketball League, and Cleveland won the first title.

In 1927 Babe Ruth smashed his sixtieth homer of the season, a feat never before accomplished.

Another event in the decade has romantic significance for me. I had moved from Brooklyn to my new church in Syracuse, New York. It has one of the most beautiful sanctuaries I have ever seen, with gigantic and artistic ecclesiastical windows composing three walls. When the sun shines through those windows, which depict the sacred story, the interior is glorious.

One Sunday in 1928 I was holding a committee meeting of university students in the front pews after morning service. I was standing facing the Genesee Street entrance when the great doors were flung open—rather impatiently, I thought—and a girl stood framed against the golden October afternoon. I did not know her name or who she was, but in that moment I knew deep inside of me that she was the girl for me. She was waiting for one of the girls attending the committee meeting.

I inquired about this young lady and discovered that she was Ruth Stafford, a senior at Syracuse University. It took me two years to persuade her to marry me. We were married at the altar of University Methodist Church on June 20, 1930, by three ministers: my father, Bishop Adna Wright Leonard, and Charles W. Flint, chancellor of Syracuse University. The Reverend Frank B. Stafford, Ruth's father, gave the bride away. Ruth's sister-in-law, Eleanor Stafford, was maid of honor, and the best man was my brother, Dr. Robert Clifford Peale.

I married a girl with a good head for business, and she has handled all business affairs in our family. As an organizer and administrator, she conceived the Foundation for Christian Living, which has serviced millions of readers with Christian literature for more than fifty years. She has been its chief executive since its inception. She also developed *Guideposts* magazine, the publication with the twelfth largest circulation in the country. She serves as the president of *Guideposts*.

Ruth is listed in *Who's Who in America*, which tells of her numerous and demanding activities. She has been chairman of the executive committee of the American Bible Society and president of the Interchurch Center, a twenty-story office building on Riverside Drive. She is also vice president for North and South America of the United Bible Societies.

We have had an exciting "team" marriage over the years, each partner doing what he or she can do best and each supporting the other. We recommend this mutual respect as the basis for long continuing love and stability in marriage.

In the twenties, two modern dictators rose in Europe. On October 30, 1922, Mussolini's Fascists marched on Rome. Some forty thousand "black shirts," as they were called, carried guns at the alert, awaiting Mussolini's order to attack Rome. But they never fired a shot, for King Victor Emmanuel III invited Mussolini to form a government. Fear of "the Communist Menace" led Italians to welcome Il Duce (the leader). He became dictator of Italy.

One of my earliest baby pictures.

My grandparents, Samuel and Laura Peale.

My parents, Anna Delaney Peale and Charles Clifford Peale, on their wedding day, October 20, 1895.

LEFT: *In early boyhood.*

BELOW: *With my brother Robert Clifford Peale (standing).*

TOP: *With my classmates at Ohio Wesleyan during World War I days. I am fifth from the right.*

BOTTOM: *My father, Charles Clifford Peale (second from right), with his three sons, (left to right) Norman Vincent, Leonard Delaney, and Robert Clifford; in 1942.*

Our wedding day, June 30, 1930, at University Methodist Church in Syracuse, N.Y. Our attendants were Ruth's sister-in-law, Eleanor Stafford, and my brother Robert Clifford Peale.

Marble Collegiate Church at Fifth Avenue and Twenty-ninth Street in New York City.

ABOVE: *In the pulpit of Marble Collegiate Church.*

RIGHT: *My great friend and associate, Dr. Smiley Blanton.*

*The Peale family in 1950: Norman, Ruth, John, Margaret,
and Elizabeth.*

The year 1923 marked the emergence of another dictator when flags burst out in Munich, bearing an insignia called the swastika. It was the mark of Adolf Hitler's National Socialist Party, which was growing in numbers. The first public conference of the Nazi party was held on January 27, 1923, and received wide support for its demand that the Versailles Treaty, ending World War I, be repealed.

The party claimed that this treaty had caused Germany's mounting economic troubles, the decline of the mark being one. For example, an egg cost 810 marks. One U.S. dollar equaled 20,000 marks. On November 12, 1923, Hitler attempted to mount a coup against the government but failed and was arrested. On December 20, 1924, Hitler received a sentence of five years in prison for attempting to topple the German government. He was pardoned after serving nine months in jail and immediately reorganized his Nazi party, which had been banned.

In 1926 Hitler published a book called *Mein Kampf* (*My Struggle*), which was a demagogic book calling for a national revival and a battle against Communism and the Jews. It became a manual for the Nazi party. In elections in September 1930 the Nazi party became the second largest party in Germany, going from 12 seats to 107 in the New Reichstag. Hitler said Germany "must rise from its ashes and get even for World War I." In July 1932 Hitler's party seats increased from 107 in the Reichstag to 229.

Hitler was received by President Von Hindenburg on January 30, 1933, and so strong was his support among the people that he was made chancellor of Germany. Two months later, on March 23, Hitler was granted dictatorial power. The Reichstag adjourned, leaving him to make laws by personal decree.

Later the same day, Goering denied newspaper reports of bodies floating in a Berlin canal. Immediately boycotts were put into effect against Jewish shop owners. Hitler completed his personal domination of Germany by outlawing all other political parties. Book-burning took place throughout the nation, destroying books that were declared un-German. "Race science" was introduced into German schools. The authorities inaugurated the policy of arresting Jews and sending them to prison camp. Ultimately, Hitler caused the murders of several million people, according to the most reliable reports. Hitler took Germany out of the League of Nations because other nations had been treating Germany like a "second-class citizen."

The story of Adolf Hitler reached a climax when German voters elected him president as well as chancellor. His power was now total.

I have detailed this story of Mussolini and Hitler to remind us of what, under certain circumstances, can happen to a country with long traditions. Also I want to show the end of dictators when circumstances changed. As the decade of the thirties passed into the forties, the Allies entered into World War II in order to contain Hitler, who apparently saw world mastery within his grasp. But the forces of freedom prevailed after the severest war in history.

Europe experienced all the horror of war: the devastated cities, the ruined economy, the holocaust of Jews, murders, and untold suffering. Then contemplate the fate of dictators: Il Duce, the leader of the Black Shirts of Italy, ended his life hanging upside down, his bullet-riddled body rotting in the hot Italian sun, dangling by his heels alongside the body of his mistress. Where was all his glory now? Facing a firing squad on April 28, 1945, he had cried even as he was shot, "Let me live and I'll give you an empire."

And what of the upstart chancellor of Germany, president and general of the armies, the would-be master of the world, who at the height of his career seemed invincible? The end of this ruthless dictator was ignominious as the Allied armies closed in on devastated Berlin. In an underground bunker, Hitler, like an animal at bay—he who had vowed to create a Reich that would last a thousand years—took his own life. His body was doused with gasoline and burned. That grim biblical statement of truth comes to mind: "The way of the transgressor is hard."

CHAPTER 4

The Unforgettable Thirties

CERTAINLY no one who lived through the Great Depression of the 1930s will ever forget those years. Everyone living at that time was affected to one degree or another, for this financial catastrophe had a worldwide effect. Those of us living in New York may have more sensitive memories of those times, for we were in the money capital of the country and, actually, of the world.

The Great Depression came with a roar on "Black Friday," October 29, 1929. It was the most disastrous day in Wall Street history in total losses, in total turnovers, and in the number of investors ruined financially. It was all the more dramatic because since 1921 the country had enjoyed a period of unprecedented prosperity. Seemingly everyone was speculating in the market "on margin," and when the call came for more payment, many suffered ruinous losses. All attempts failed to restore the market to a stable condition. Stocks continued to decline. The noted British economist John Maynard Keynes, when asked if he could point to any historical period that equaled the Great Depression replied, "Yes, it was called the Dark Ages and lasted four hundred years. This one lasted only a few years, but it was a dark, sad end for the decade of the twenties that had been described as 'roaring.'"

More than a quarter of the work force was out of jobs and never for ten years did unemployment drop much below 15 percent. Hundreds of thousands of farmers lost their land. Millions of families accustomed to security, even affluence, experienced deprivation and terrifying fear for the first time.

Businesses closed, shop windows were boarded up, thousands walked the streets futilely looking for jobs. Soup kitchens to feed the hungry were set up, and often, in the long lines of those waiting to be fed, were well-dressed persons who obviously had seen prosperous days.

I was living in Syracuse when all this started, and the depression quickly came home to me as the income of the church dried up. My personal income was cut several times. Just about everyone was experiencing cuts in salaries and wages. It becomes more significant, however, when one remembers that the high for the Dow Jones Industrial Average in 1929 was 381.2. The low was 198.7. The destruction of the market, in spite of all one hears about Black Friday, took some time. The worst year was 1932, when the high was 88.8.

The financial depression was equaled by a depression of spirit. I recall meeting one of the outstanding business leaders of Syracuse on the street, and when I asked what he thought of the situation, he replied glumly, "This has been a great country, but the United States will never experience prosperity again."

Later, at a Rotary Club meeting, the speaker—a prominent and widely read economist—said in effect that America would have to get used to a permanently lower standard of living, that looking into the future, we would never again enjoy prosperity. Well, "never" is a long time, and negative, gloomy appraisals should not be taken too seriously. By the end of the 1930s, the

United States finally began to shake off depression and went to work and found new levels of living.

We also began to recover our American attitudes of faith in God and in country. The historic ability of Americans to take up their belts, to smile and go on working, asserted itself, and we started the trek back up. I was in this with everyone else. I had nothing but a shrunken salary, and yet, taking stock, I had a young, positive-thinking and faith-believing wife, and I had a job comforting and encouraging people. So I kept plugging and working and believing. Those three principles will get you through anything—keep on plugging, working, and believing.

In March of 1932 Syracuse was still locked in one of the severest winters upstate New York had experienced in my memory. When an invitation came to preach one Sunday in the Marble Collegiate Church on Fifth Avenue in New York City, I was inclined to accept it. When I told Ruth about the invitation, she responded with enthusiasm. "No way are we going to pass up a weekend in New York, especially since it means getting away from this rugged weather for a few days."

So on March 13, 1932, I preached in this historic Fifth Avenue church, which was founded way back in 1628 by Dutch settlers when New York was a little village called New Amsterdam. Now the congregation had declined, for it had been without a full-time pastor for three years. I spoke to 201 persons at the morning service and 215 in the evening. They had an usher who had been instructed to count the congregation at every service, for there had been a movement to discontinue the church.

The next Sunday, back in my full church in Syracuse, I was startled to notice a couple of men whom I had met the previous Sunday, officials of the New York church. And they were also in the congregation at the evening service. Afterward they approached me for a meeting and subsequently called me to their church. I told them of an invitation from Dr. Elmer Ellsworth Helms, pastor of the First Methodist Episcopal Church (the present name of this denomination is The United Methodist Church) in Los Angeles. His was a huge church, standing at the downtown corner of Eighth and Hope Streets. At that time, due to the energy and pulpit power of Dr. Helms, the church was said to have the largest Methodist congregation in the world. Indeed it was a vast structure seating thirty-three hundred persons in the main sanctuary, which was furnished with individual theater-type seats rather than pews. The church was invariably packed whenever he preached.

Dr. Helms had asked me to preach at all services during the month of May in 1932. I discovered later that, since he was coming up to retirement, he wanted me to succeed him and was "showing me off" to the congregation, hoping the official board would ask me to be their pastor.

The men from Marble said that since they were offering me a lifetime contract, a couple of months would not make a difference.

Ruth and I had a pleasant month at the Los Angeles church and received a unanimous invitation to be their permanent minister. Back home in Syracuse we debated the question. Which call should we accept, or should we stay in Syracuse? This inability to arrive at a decision went on day after day. One day at noon I went home to lunch, and Ruth, ever decisive, said, "We are going to decide this matter before you leave this house."

So we went into the living room and Ruth, also a firm believer in divine guidance, said, "We are going to stay in prayer until God gives us His answer."

Never before or since, except one time when our son, John, hovered between life and death in a hospital in North Carolina, have I spent so long a time continuously in an attitude of prayer. We told God we wanted only to do what He wanted us to do if He would tell us. And He did just that. For suddenly I knew definitely.

Finally, Ruth asked, "Have you an answer?"

And I said, "Yes, I have."

And then I asked her if she had received an answer, and she said that she had. "What is your answer?" I asked.

"Nothing doing," she replied. "This is your decision, and I'll go wherever you go."

I said, "God wants us to go to New York."

She immediately became brisk and businesslike. "That's my answer, too. Pick up that phone and call Mr. Denison [chairman of the Marble board] and tell him you accept their call."

I did so, and immediately upon conveying the message of acceptance, I had a strong inner feeling of peace that I had done the right thing. Not once in the fifty-two years that I was minister of the New York church, not even when the going was a bit rough, did I feel otherwise.

A sequel to all this occurred in the fall of 1989, about fifty-seven years after I had preached in Los Angeles for a month. Ruth and I had lunch with friends in downtown Los Angeles. As we were driving to our hotel I asked, "Aren't we near Eighth and Hope? Please drive by that corner and let's look at 'the old church.'" We stopped under street signs that read "Eighth and Hope." But I'm sad to say that where the great church had stood, thronged by people, a big parking lot now stood.

My friend explained, "Nobody lives in this neighborhood anymore."

As we drove away, Ruth and I experienced mingled feelings of sadness and gratitude for God's guidance in our lives.

On Sunday evening, October 2, 1932, I was installed as the minister of the Marble Collegiate Church, Fifth Avenue and Twenty-ninth Street, New York City.

My father gave me the charge that night, telling me, as I

stood before him in the presence of a great congregation, "I am proud of you, my son. You have never disappointed me, and you will not disappoint me now." And then he put some humor into a solemn occasion when he told that he, a one-time doctor of medicine, personally delivered me at my birth, adding, "You were yelling then and have been yelling ever since." Ruth, my young and beautiful wife, was seated with Mother in the "Pastor's Pew," so indicated by a silver plaque. Charles Phillip, church clerk for many years, told me that night, "We called you to this church really because we were so charmed by Ruth."

When all the people had gone that night, I found Mother outside the Fifth Avenue entrance of the church with her hand on one of the huge marble blocks of which the church is built. She was weeping. "What's the matter, Mother?" I asked.

She said, "This church is so strong. Always keep it strong, Norman." And that I tried to do for the fifty-two years I served as its minister.

America was growing even during the greatest depression in history. The federal census of 1930 indicated that the population of the United States was now 122.7 million, a dramatic increase of 30 million people over the almost 92 million counted in the 1910 census. New York City was still number one. The most spectacular growth was in the far West, with Los Angeles rated number five among the nation's cities. Among the states, Arizona experienced the most rapid growth—435,000 lived there, representing an increase of 100,000 in a decade.

The signs of the times included such things as new food items; Wonder Bread and Mott's Applesauce, for instance, were now on our table. Pan Am was the largest air carrier, having merged with two smaller lines. New airlines were American, Braniff, Trans World, and United.

The cost of living in the thirties is indicated by the following prices:

A three-bedroom home could be bought for $5,000.

The average annual income was $1,552.

A new Ford car cost $550.

One loaf of bread cost nine cents.

One gallon of gas, twenty cents.

One gallon of milk, fifty cents.

One pound of bacon cost forty-three cents.

And at the time we thought things were high!

Many new inventions made their appearance—windshield wipers, for instance. Children and older people as well began to hear on radio a story featuring a masked hero and a fiery horse, with great speed, a cloud of dust, and a hearty, "Hi ho, Silver, the Lone Ranger rides again!" Bishop Fulton J. Sheen was fascinating multitudes with his radio and, later, TV broadcasts. Bobby Jones was grand slam golfing champion, winning in a single year the U.S. Open, the British Open, the British Amateur, and the U.S. Amateur in 1930. In all, Bobby Jones captured thirteen championships in fourteen years.

But there were ominous events also. You couldn't possibly forget the depression or the great drought. Congress in 1930 appropriated $45 million for drought relief to help farmers with loans and to feed livestock. Senator Heflin of Alabama made a speech in the Senate calling attention to starving people: "Striking out human food and buying food for livestock puts hogs above humans and mules above men." Congress, at President Hoover's insistence, appropriated $116 million to put the unemployed back to work on emergency public work projects in the wake of the market crash.

In 1931 it was reported to Congress that there were between 4 and 5 million jobless in the nation, and President Nicholas Murray Butler of Columbia University warned that the unprecedented unemployment situation represented a "danger to the social order."

More than three hundred impoverished farmers stormed into an Alabama town shouting, "We want food," and threatening to loot the stores unless they got food for their children. Agencies, there to help in the economic crisis, were compelled to say they had no food to dole out. Local merchants, themselves in difficulty, were so moved by this human need that they met and agreed to give food to all the suffering people.

But along with all these troubles the nation continued its usual life. For example, the great George Washington Bridge over the Hudson River from New York to New Jersey, begun in 1927, was opened on October 27, 1931, as the longest suspension bridge in the world. A world record was set in July of 1933 when Wiley Post circumnavigated the world in seven days, eighteen hours, and forty-nine and a half minutes. And Al Capone, Chicago gangster, finally landed in jail as a tax dodger and was sentenced to an eleven-year prison term on October 17, 1931.

I knew President Herbert Hoover personally and admired him. He was a great, compassionate, caring man who had the misfortune to be chief executive of this nation when the people understandably were intensely disturbed by economic conditions. Hoover said, "The taxpayer is now contributing to the livelihood of 10 million of our citizens. The depression is caused by a lack of confidence. A first step toward economic recovery involves reestablishment of the flow of credit, which is the basis of our economic life." He believed that when business is good, full employment follows.

After his presidency Hoover came, at my invitation, to the church to address a dinner meeting of the Men's League. As I watched a former president of the United States talk to a group of men in a church basement no differently than he would talk to thousands, I had a feeling of affection for this man who, though revered by some, was reviled and hated by many.

I asked him once how he never answered back when he was unjustly condemned and always preserved a calm and dignified composure. He answered simply, "I am a Quaker." And I knew exactly what he meant. Quakers cultivate "peace at the center," and Herbert Hoover had that ineffable peace.

Once I called at the Mark Hopkins Hotel in San Francisco to see him. Mr. Hoover had said he would be there for some time, working on a book, and invited me to come to see him. I found him hard at work, surrounded by papers on which he had made notes. I observed that they were not scattered about in disorder but were arranged in systematic fashion. When I commented on his neatness and order he said, "Oh, you see, I am an engineer."

I inquired about the subject matter of his book, and he told me he was writing on the life of Woodrow Wilson. When I expressed a bit of surprise that a former Republican president was writing on the life of a former Democratic president, he replied, "Woodrow Wilson was one of our greatest Americans." So was Herbert Hoover, in my opinion. I find it interesting that Presidents Wilson and Hoover, and even Abraham Lincoln, were highly misunderstood in their lifetime and suffered contumely.

I asked Mr. Hoover once the secret of his success in life, rising from a poor orphan boy to president. His reply was in another one of those short sentences. "I was raised by older people. Maybe I absorbed some of their knowledge." He was a deeply religious man. My last memory of him is when I preached one Sunday morning in the little country church on Quaker Hill in Pawling, New York. In the pews before me were notables of New York City business and publishing, including the famous broadcaster Lowell Thomas, Governor Thomas E. Dewey, and former President Herbert Hoover. Afterward at dinner at Lowell's beautiful home nearby, Mr. Hoover was good enough to speak kindly about my sermon of the morning and conclude with another of his terse remarks, though this was expressed with deep feeling: "My faith has helped me all through life."

I have called this chapter "The Unforgettable Thirties." And one reason this era cannot be forgotten is that new inventions and products were coming out fast: Alka Seltzer, synthetic rubber, dry ice, Schick shavers, infrared photography, and air-conditioning. Remember how I said I suffered in those hot summers as a boy?

Just up the avenue from my church, at Fifth Avenue and Thirty-fourth Street, the tallest building in the world, the Empire State Building, was opened. The moving spirit in erecting this building was the great governor of the State of New York, Alfred E. Smith. In Washington, President Hoover pushed a button that turned on the lights in the building.

I recall reading in newspapers at the time that the Empire State Building was so wonderful that "it is likely that the building will not soon be surpassed. It is also likely to exist along with the pyramids of Egypt as a testimony to the building skills of the human race." So went the exaggerated praises of an admittedly great building.

I knew Governor Al Smith well and admired him greatly. He once ran for president. A poor boy from the lower East Side, he became one of the greatest Americans of his time. Once in his office in the Empire State Building, Al Smith, who was a dedicated Catholic, said to me, "Ever hear of the Protestant woman who believed in every word in the Protestant Bible? Once when she wanted to know what to do, she closed her eyes and opened the Bible and put her finger down on the page. She opened her eyes and read the verse which said, 'And Judas went out and hanged himself.' She had to admit that was not the guidance she needed so tried it again and this time she read, 'Go and do thou likewise.'" Governor Smith laughed uproariously. He was one of the most interesting and likeable public men I have known.

Still, when the Empire State Building was opened, it was only about half rented, with lots of empty space. The depression was still on and would continue awhile. About this time America's great humorist Will Rogers, the Bob Hope of that era and one of the best-loved men in the history of the United States, said, referring to the depression, "We are the first nation to go to the poorhouse in an automobile." Once he met President Calvin Coolidge. Rogers acted puzzled saying, "I didn't get the name." Coolidge for once is reported to have burst into laughter.

When we were living in Syracuse, a son of one of my church members, a widowed mother, got into trouble and was in prison. The district attorney and the judge who sentenced him thought there were perhaps "mitigating circumstances," but only the governor could lift a sentence in this case and advised me, if I felt I should take action, to see Governor Franklin D. Roosevelt.

I had met the governor only briefly when he was at Quaker Hill as a guest of Lowell Thomas, but I saw him about this case and noted how charming was his personality. He recounted at some length a trip he had just made throughout the state with particular reference to the "beautiful little country churches" he had seen. I found this narrative very interesting, especially the manner in which he told it. I figured he was especially nice to me, for he understood my pastoral concern for the mother and son and, not wanting to pardon the boy who he felt was guilty, he "let me down easy." He had the rare ability to say no and leave one not feeling too bad about it.

The next time I saw Franklin D. Roosevelt, he greeted me pleasantly but made no reference to the case about which I had seen him earlier.

Statistics told an ugly story in the depression era. The jobless rate in some cities reached the staggering figure of 50 percent. At least 2 million people wandered the country as vagrants. A well-known writer of the era referred to "the breakdown of the romance of business." Another lesser known writer painted a sad word picture of the "defeated, discouraged, hopeless men and women, cringing and bowing as they come to ask for public aid." He called it the "descent from respectability."

The Reverend James R. Cox led some eighteen thousand unemployed men from Pittsburgh to Washington—"Cox's Army," it was called. They asked the president and Congress for relief from destitution, pointing out on January 6, 1932, that wages had fallen off 60 percent since the market crash that signaled the Great Depression.

A poignant news story dated July 28, 1932, tells of a "Bonus Army" of some nine thousand former servicemen marching on Washington. Federal troops commanded by Douglas MacArthur were ordered by the president to forcibly remove the Bonus Army from the capital. The troops burned the shacks set up by the Bonus Army. MacArthur is reported to have said that "he felt revolution in the air." His aide, Major Dwight D. Eisenhower, said, "It was a pitiful scene that should not have been permitted to happen. The Bonus Army, so-called, was composed of unemployed veterans of World War I who were demanding that the bonus promised them for service in the war be paid to them immediately."

President Hoover, coping valiantly with the depression situation, in July 1932 gave the Reconstruction Finance Corporation power to lend $1.8 billion to the states for the relief of the homeless and the unemployed, but it was not enough.

In the unforgettable thirties also came the abduction of the Lindbergh baby. On March 1, 1932, the twenty-month-old son of Colonel and Mrs. Charles A. Lindbergh was kidnapped from his nursery in the home of his parents near Hopewell, New Jersey. His name was Charles A. Lindbergh, Jr.

Only muddy footprints were found in the nursery. Pinned to the windowsill was a note demanding $50,000 ransom, which Colonel Lindbergh said he would willingly pay, but no instructions were given about how to deliver the ransom.

President Hoover ordered more than one hundred thousand officers to search the entire eastern seaboard. Not until May 12 was the child's body discovered in a shallow grave, less than five miles from his home.

A doctor who conducted an autopsy said that the baby had been brutally murdered soon after the kidnapping. Bruno Hauptmann, an illegal immigrant from Germany, was eventually charged, found guilty on largely circumstantial evidence, and executed in the electric chair in 1936.

In the fall of the year 1932 the debonair Mayor Jimmy Walker of New York City resigned his office amidst charges of scandal. I knew Jimmy Walker, a charming fellow whom the newspapers credited with a "comprehensive subway system and a good sanitation department." That he had ability was not denied.

Franklin D. Roosevelt, the nominee of the Democratic party, was elected president in the 1932 election.

I was facing, in these depression times, my own minor depression in my new job at Marble Collegiate Church in New York City. I listened to FDR, as the newspapers called the new president, as he gave his first inaugural address (at the last inauguration to be held in March). In that address he got off a phrase that impressed me as a great statement for a public figure to make, particularly in the difficult times we were then experiencing. Roosevelt said, "The only thing we have to fear is fear itself," which is a positive truth. Some years later the famous writer Napoleon Hill, who served at the time as a speechwriter for Roosevelt, told me that he was the author of that great statement.

Well, I was giving sermons against the blanket of fear resting over the country, saying that there are two great forces available to people: fear is one great power, but there is one force more powerful than fear, and that is faith. And I pointed out that faith can always destroy fear because faith is rational and enables one to think factually, objectively, intelligently, with a clear and uncluttered mind free of the shadowy phantoms of fear. Therefore, I agreed with FDR's powerful statement that "the only thing we have to fear is fear itself."

Now about my "minor" depression. It seemed anything but minor to me at the time. I had a church that seated sixteen hundred people but had a congregation of only two hundred. Those empty pews haunted me. Pews are for human bodies to sit in, I reasoned, and the humans on the city streets needed to be in these pews to recover the only factor that can dissipate their fears, namely faith. So I preached sermon after sermon on faith, giving it other names like "belief in God" and then "belief in yourself," "belief in the future, your future." I called it the "power of positive thinking," unknowingly using a title later to be put on a book.

Following our first year of dealing with the dismal condition of the Marble Collegiate Church, in the summer of 1933 Ruth and I took our vacation in England. We settled down in the town of Keswick in the Lake District, a region of hills and lakes, renowned for charm and beauty and filled with historic places connected with the great figures of English literature.

But I was restless and depressed about the church back in New York. It seemed a hopeless situation; why had I ever taken on such a job anyway? In a gloomy manner I poured my woes into the ears of my happy and positive young wife. The Station Hotel, in which we were staying, was surrounded by a beautiful formal English garden. Charming old hedges and venerable trees and glorious beds of flowers made it a place of serenity. We strolled its graveled walks and sat on its benches, particularly one at the far end of the garden.

It was while we sat on this bench that one of the determinative experiences of my life occurred, one that dramatically changed me and my total existence. It was vital to everything that happened afterward in my personal history. As I sat there giving vent to all my discouragement and negative thoughts, Ruth proceeded to do a masterful job of therapy upon me. Normally Ruth is a kindly and good-tempered lady, but at that moment she became firm and authoritative, psychologically and spiritually.

"You," she said, "are not only my husband, you are also my pastor, and in the latter department I'm frank to say I am becoming increasingly disappointed in you. I hear you from the pulpit talking about faith and trust in God's wondrous power. But now I hear from you no faith or trust at all. You just whine your defeat. And to put it bluntly, what you need is a deep spiritual experience. You need to be converted."

"I have been converted," I expostulated.

"Well, it didn't take," she snapped, "so you had better get really converted."

We sat in deep silence, broken finally by her statement that she was not going to leave that bench, nor was I, until I had found the Lord in such depth that I became a remade person. "How do I do that?" I asked meekly.

"You, a pastor, ask me how you do it?" she commented. "Tell the Lord you are totally lost, without strength, that you have no power within yourself, and that you are humbly throwing yourself on His divine mercy and that you are asking Him to change you now."

She took my hand in a strong grip. "Ask Him now aloud, and I am praying for you, too." So in a stumbling sort of way, I confessed all my weaknesses, entreating the Lord to come to me, defeated as I was. I kept repeating this, surrendering, self-giving, and I prayed with great intensity. And the prayer was answered instantly. I began to feel warm all over from the crown of my head to my feet. Joy such as I had never known welled up within me, intermingled with tears. I laughed and cried. Leaping to my feet, I paced up and down excitedly.

"It's wonderful!" I cried, "Wonderful, glorious! He has answered me. He is in my heart, my mind. Nothing can defeat me now, not that church or anything. I want to get back to work. We are going to have a wonderful time from here on in. Tell you what," I said. "Let's go back to New York right now and tackle that job with power. We don't need any more vacation."

Ruth said with mock despair, "Oh, my, I've gone too far with this!" But she, as excited as I, went to pack at once, and a thrilled young couple were soon on their way back to dismal old Fifth Avenue and Twenty-ninth Street. But it was no longer dismal, for we saw the problem in a different spirit and through new eyes. Sure, there were lots of difficulties, but never again was I really down, and that old deteriorating church became filled with new life and faith and joy and power and people. From that low point it started a strong upward movement toward the top, where it has been ever since. In such manner does the good Lord work when given the chance to take over a life, especially when the subject has such a strong, believing, wise, and loving wife.

Years later I was a guest on Ralph Edwards's famous TV show "This Is Your Life." You may recall that the guest was always brought onto the show in Hollywood by subterfuge;

therefore, I was totally unprepared for questions. But in front of a big studio audience and millions of viewers, when Ralph asked me to state the greatest thing that had ever happened to me, I instantly told of my experience with the astonishing grace of God on a bench in a garden in England.

I came back from that English garden bench and delivered confident, positive, enthusiastic messages that began to draw people. At first a trickle of people came, and finally the church filled up so that ultimately we were using overflow rooms. Then we went to duplicate services. The crowds continued to come, and today, six years after I retired from Marble, capacity congregations crowd the church to hear Dr. Arthur Caliandro preach the gospel that faith in God will destroy fear and every other evil thing that draws off the joy of life.

Another, but different, event happened. About eleven-thirty on the night of November 17, 1933, our eldest child, Margaret Ann Peale, was born at Doctor's Hospital in New York City. I sat in the lounge all evening, while one expectant father after another had his baby delivered, received congratulations, and took his relieved departure. Finally, only one other man and I remained. We got very friendly as we talked. He told me that he had been saying his Jewish prayers all evening. I responded that my Protestant prayers were also going up to God.

Then a nurse appeared in the doorway. We both expectantly leaped to our feet. She said to my friend, "Congratulations! You have a beautiful, healthy baby girl."

"That's because I thought you needed a Protestant prayer," I said. We both laughed and shook hands. I never saw him again, but we exchanged letters on the anniversary of this night until his death many years later.

Then I sat alone sending more prayers to God. About eleven-thirty the same nurse appeared, with the same announcement. "Congratulations! You have a beautiful, healthy baby girl." I followed her to look through a window at a baby crying forcefully.

"Has she everything—ten fingers, ten toes, two eyes, etc?" I asked. She nodded and smiled warmly.

Next I saw Ruth. I expected her for once to be done in. But she was sprightly enough to tell me to go home and get a good night's sleep. I drove down to our home at 25 Fifth Avenue, saying to myself, "What do you know about that? I'm a father!" Passing an attractive restaurant on Lexington Avenue, I rationalized that my evening's work had tired me and I certainly deserved a midnight snack of ample proportion, which, indeed, I did enjoy.

Margaret is now the wife of the Reverend Paul F. Everett and is still "beautiful and healthy" as on that unforgettable night so many years ago.

A great and historic event took place on November 7, 1933, when the Fusion candidate for mayor of New York City, former congressman Fiorello H. LaGuardia, was overwhelmingly elected. He resoundingly wrestled long-held control of the city from Tammany Hall in the largest voter turnout in the city's history.

I personally knew Mayor LaGuardia, for whom the airport is named. He was called the "Little Flower," but he was a strong, incorruptible man. A certain teenger worked for him one summer when he was still congressman. She had a low self-esteem because she was short, only four feet, eleven inches. This self-depreciation must have showed when, by chance, she was with Mr. LaGuardia one day in an elevator, for he said, "Young lady, you listen to me, for I know what I'm talking about. Trust God and believe in yourself and you can do anything."

As he stepped from the elevator, she thought, *Why, he is short, too.* He was five feet, two inches. But she saw him as a giant of a man. He was really that.

This was the decade of Senator Huey P. Long of Louisiana,

who was called the "Kingfish." He campaigned for a redistribution of wealth and was author of the book *Every Man a King.* He had a spellbinding style of speaking in the Senate, the public platform, and even on radio. Thousands tuned in to hear him say, "Here's Huey Long. I'm on the air. I'm not going to say much worth listening to for awhile. Call up your friends and say, 'Huey is on the radio.'" By such appeals he mustered an audience of thousands. After a meteoric career, Huey Long died by an assassin's bullet in 1935.

The Prohibition law was repealed fourteen years after it began with the adoption of the Twenty-first Amendment. President Hoover called it "a noble experiment," and repeal was a major plank in the Roosevelt campaign. America's first aircraft carrier, the USS *Ranger,* was launched. The famed gangster John Dillinger, labeled "public enemy number one," was shot as he left a Chicago movie house on July 22, 1934. Lawmen gunned down Bonnie and Clyde, both in their twenties, near Ruston, Louisiana, on May 23, 1934. They were accused of robbing banks and committing multiple murders.

Also in 1934, a calamitous drought gripped the Midwest. After nine months without rain, farmers were in a state of panic. Farm prices fell more than 50 percent in three or four years; farmers forcibly resisted attempted foreclosures. An official of the Farm Bureau Federation said, "Unless something is done for the American farmer, we will have revolution in the countryside in less than twelve months."

But the idea that farmers would engage in revolution proved to be far too pessimistic. Loyal to their government, they suffered unimaginably but did not revolt. A year later the drought and the depression were still devastating. At least half of Iowa's farmers are said to have lost their land. Dust storms of 1933 and 1934 continued in Texas and Oklahoma and gradually covered almost all the West. Vast areas of the land were termed the "Dust Bowl." Tremendous clouds of dust obscured the sun as far east as the Appalachian Mountains. On the great plains of the West the dust drifted up against fences like snow in winter.

The roads of the Midwest were filled with financially ruined farmers, their old cars loaded with their few belongings, moving ever westward to California, trying to escape the ravages of the dust storms. But American farmers come of hardy stock, and many stuck it out, fortified by faith, prayer, and ingenuity. Two illustrations come to mind.

My wife, Ruth, in her capacity as president of the Women's Board of Domestic Missions of our denomination, was at a meeting in the Dust Bowl, where at a luncheon in a church she sat across from a farmer. Noticing his gnarled hands, she asked him about his crops. He was a man of few words, "Not good, ma'am," he said. "We had dust storms and thousands of grasshoppers, and I saved only 10 percent of my crops." Then he added, "My brother lost everything."

The enormity of his suffering saddened her and she asked, "What did you do?"

His answer was classic. "Why, ma'am, I just aimed to forget it."

Two of my friends, Ted and Dorothy Husted, bought a little drugstore in the village of Wall, South Dakota. In a time of drought, dust, and depression, they were embarking on a risky venture. But they were believing Christians, and they bought the store in Wall because the village had a Catholic church. But customers were few and far between. Cars were passing by their store in the intense heat through clouds of swirling dust. Dorothy sat looking through the window at the passing cars. The question was how to get some of them to come in. She prayed for an idea, and her prayers were answered. Of course, none of these cars had air-conditioning; that was a comfort yet to be. So driver and passengers drove with "tongues hanging out."

"Ted," she called, "make two signs reading: Ice Water Free at Wall Drugstore, Wall, South Dakota. Put them up twenty miles on either side of Wall." Then he made two more signs to be put up at ten miles: Hold on. It's only ten miles to Wall and free ice water. He kept putting up signs farther and farther from Wall, in every direction, and finally he even had a sign at Albany, New York, hundreds of miles from South Dakota.

People began to stop and come in. Many bought a few other things. The Wall Drugstore ultimately became one of the greatest successes in the drugstore business, serving hundreds of people daily. It's a prize illustration of the power of prayer, believing, and thinking to turn a situation around, however hopeless. Americans have had many trials and not a few tribulations, but they always, and I mean always, overcome. And why? They have faith in God, in their country, and in themselves. That's why!

In New York City, we were in trouble. As mentioned before, the depression was our problem, and I was preaching every Sunday: trust God, have faith, stick it out, be a believer in the good heavenly Father, in your country, and in yourself. These were encouraging, positive messages. This preaching of solid biblical truths, this sound psychology based on common sense and faith in God's goodness, brought ever-increasing numbers of people to the church services. Then I was inundated with requests for pastoral counseling, and I saw and listened to every troubled person who came. Human problems are always with us, but at that time they were accentuated by the fear, hopelessness, and despair caused by the depression.

I was ill prepared for the problems posed in these sessions. I had graduated from two educational institutions plus a graduate school, but in them I had had only scanty training in psychology. And, of course, I had no training in psychiatry and none in the science of counseling.

But I loved these people who came saying, "This is my problem." I cared and I listened patiently. But then I began to be suspicious that deeper problems often lay beneath the patient's assumptions about his or her problem. I decided that I needed help and professional understanding.

I went to the secretary of the New York County Medical Association, Dr. Iago Goldston. I found him to be a very kindly and understanding man. He promised to look for a psychiatrist to meet my specifications, a caring, well-prepared doctor, a Christian, one who could help a Christian minister. He had to be a believer and be of the highest professionalism.

Dr. Goldston telephoned me a few days later. "I think we have just the man you want." He invited me to lunch at the Harvard Club to meet him. Thus it was that I found Dr. Smiley Blanton, the person who would be my associate and friend for many years until his death. He was one of the most outstanding psychiatrists of the century.

Dr. Blanton listened to my problem and finally asked a seemingly irrelevant question, considering the conversation. It was, "Do you believe in prayer?" Without giving me time to answer, for he knew the answer, he told me that for a long time he had been praying that he would meet a pastor with whom he could team up in a relationship of pastoral therapy and psychological science. Up to that time he knew of no such relationship: indeed, all too often there existed a strained feeling, if not actual hostility, between pastors and psychiatrists. Actually, our meeting marked the beginning of a turnaround, what Dr. Blanton later called the greatest advance in pastoral treatment in centuries.

We started with Dr. Blanton's coming to my office or having lunch or dinner with me every week to discuss particular cases that I had at the moment. Soon he became so interested that he was giving as much time as he could take away from his private practice. And always he came to the church for these interviews. He said, "God heals the patient. I'm only His agent." He was always insistent on the spiritual reality of healing. He said, "I help the patient to understand why he does what he does. Then you, the pastor, help him—in a leap of faith—to do with God's help what he now knows he should do."

Soon Smiley Blanton was bringing younger psychiatrists to help with treatment. They gave freely of their time, for our caseload was increasing. Soon it outgrew the church building, and we tried a couple of other locations, but Dr. Blanton was unhappy about them. Finally the church bought a building adjoining the church, at 3 West Twenty-ninth Street, where we established offices. He was satisfied, saying, "We must always work under the eaves of God's house, for He is the great Healer of His children."

Smiley always described himself as a "hillbilly Methodist from Tennessee." He was raised in a rural district, went to Vanderbilt University, studied under Dr. Sigmund Freud in Vienna, and served on the staff of the College of Physicians and Surgeons in London. Later he was a professor at the University of Wisconsin. He wrote learned books on psychiatry and was the great authority on stuttering, along with Margaret, his wife, who was equally scholarly.

Together, in 1938, we founded the Institute of Religion and Health, now called "The Blanton Peale Institute." It is a three-year training program for pastors, priests, and rabbis, and includes a fully staffed clinic. It is recognized in the mental health field as one of the finest programs because of its superior faculty and outstanding accomplishments. Graduates of The Blanton Peale Institute are practicing all over the United States, helping thousands of people with their emphasis on the healing partnership of religion and psychiatry.

Smiley Blanton was one of the truly great men I have known,

genuinely wise, caring, and kindly. I asked him once what basic characteristics one must have to be a great psychiatrist. His reply was, "Insight and love." He pointed out that insight is not acquired or taught in a university. If you have it, then it can be trained. And to love the patient is necessary despite the reactions that may come in the healing process.

Smiley was finally stricken when he was walking alone on lower Broadway. Finding no other place, he sat on a curb with crowds passing by. A policeman took him to the hospital, where our mutual physician, Dr. Louis Faugeres Bishop, attended him. He died that night. Louis telephoned me. "Smiley's kind old heart just wore out doing good," he said.

In my ninety-two years of life I have been privileged to know many people in all walks and activities, from the famous to the humble, and I'm grateful for all of them, for I've learned something of value from each. I go on the theory that every human being has his or her own story, and everyone can convey a bit of wisdom. I am a part of all I have ever met.

I accepted an invitation to speak one night in 1934 in a club in uptown New York at a meeting of "rising young New York businessmen." Some three hundred of them were present. For the most part I judged they were in their thirties or early forties, an attractive crowd of intelligent young men.

At the head table I was seated between interesting fellows. And with an eye to business as well as to make conversation, I said to the man on my left, "Where do you go to church?" Just like that. You could tell that it rather astonished him.

"Oh," he replied when he had recovered, "my father and grandfather were Presbyterians."

"But," I rejoined, "you mistook my question. I didn't ask about your father or grandfather." I was about to let the matter pass, but he continued.

"You see, the tension is pretty terrible in business these days, and I'm tired on Sunday. A game of golf relaxes me, but my wife represents us both at church."

"OK, I understand," I replied.

Turning then to the man on my right, who was running the meeting, I asked him right out of the blue, "Where do you go to church?"

He didn't react as the first man had. He only gulped and said, "I'm a nonactive Episcopalian who thinks church is just right for wives and kids, but you see, on Sundays I owe it to my job to wade through the Sunday paper."

"Wade through is about right," I agreed.

Then, sensing he was a thoughtful fellow, I asked, "You've got about three hundred rising young executives here. How many would you say are practicing Christians, church-going men?"

He drew Fred, my other seatmate, into the calculation and together they concluded about 25 percent of them.

For some reason that disturbed me so much that after the meeting I walked all the way from Fifty-fifth to Tenth Street, where I lived, about forty blocks, more than two miles. "Who are these guys," I fumed, "to look disparagingly on Christianity, which generated the free enterprise system and puts strength into the very social order that affords them business opportunity?"

Next morning I went to see Harold Peat, a friend who operated a speaking agency. "Hal," I said, having told him my experience of the night before, "I want you to get me a convention engagement to reach businessmen."

"Sure," he said, "only you can't preach sermons to secular crowds. But having heard many of your sermons, I would say you could turn them into a speech."

Soon he dated me up for a county convention upstate.

A farmer met me at the train. "Funny thing that the boys

have you, a preacher, to make the main speech." After the meeting, as we returned to the train station, the same farmer said, "You were not too bad. In fact, you were pretty good. Tell you what. You could make a sermon out of that speech." I never did tell him that the speech was made from a sermon. Since that time, for about sixty years, I've spoken in every state and to many national business conventions in the United States and in every province of Canada and have had numerous speaking trips overseas.

Woodrow Wilson's secretary of state, Bainbridge Colby, was a great friend of mine. He was aristocratic in looks and in dress, with mannerisms of the old school. He spoke with a meticulous upper-class diction. He telephoned me late one afternoon in the autumn of 1935 and said, "Norman, I have severe laryngitis and cannot speak much above a whisper, as you will note." Then he told me he wanted me to substitute for him at the American Institute of Speech dinner at the Waldorf that very night. He said there would be about a thousand speech experts and speech teachers from all parts of the country.

I sputtered that no one could take the place of the great Bainbridge Colby, certainly not I, and that I had insufficient time to prepare.

"But," he said, "old boy, I'm counting on you," and rang off.

So dutifully I went to the dinner and did my best. I do not remember the subject matter, which was put together on the run. Next morning the newspaper, in reporting the meeting, said, "Speech ranged all the way from Mrs. Richard Mansfield's delightful old-stage English to the broad 'Ohioese' of Dr. Peale."

And so the unforgettable thirties went along. Father Charles Coughlin, a fiery radio priest-turned-politician, attracted millions to his "National Union for Social Justice" before being eventually forbidden to publish his anti-Semitic publication,

Social Justice. The first big-league baseball game under lights was played in Cincinnati on May 24, 1935. The Social Security law was adopted. Dale Carnegie published his famous book *How to Win Friends and Influence People.* And, in 1936, FDR defeated Governor Alf Landon in the presidential election.

Alcoholics Anonymous, which was to help thousands, was formed by Bill W. I knew Bill Wilson well and admired him. I told him once he had helped more people than anyone else alive. I remember Bill as a rather dapper and well-dressed young man of extraordinary force of personality, though quiet and somewhat self-effacing.

He told me of what he described as "the ruinous effect" alcohol was having on him. "I knew I had to get free from it," he said. In desperation he went out and walked and walked aimlessly but fast. Presently he found himself at the top of a hill where the wind was blowing hard. It was whipping across the hilltop, sweeping it clean of leaves and catching up clouds of dust.

"O God," he prayed, "I have no strength in me. Like that wind, let Your powerful Spirit blow through my mind, driving out all of my weakness." Bill believed that fervent prayer would be answered. And it was. "I could actually feel something blowing it all away, leaving me clean."

In 1935 American Airlines unveiled its new passenger plane, the DC-3. The first flight I ever took was on an old DC-3, from Harrisburg, Pennsylvania, to what was called at the time Idlewild Airport in New York. When President Kennedy was assassinated, Mayor Robert Wagner of New York changed the name of the airport to Kennedy in his honor.

The DC-3, as I remember it, was a small plane seating about twenty-one persons. It had two seats on either side. One boarded from the rear and had to walk up quite an incline. It was a propeller plane, of course. When it had taxied to the end of the runway, the pilot revved up the motors for quite a long time. For its day, it was a powerful, competent plane and was called "the workhorse of the skies."

I took many a flight on the DC-3, and one flight I will never forget. I had a speaking engagement in McAllen, Texas. Our plane made stops in Corpus Christi and Brownsville before reaching McAllen. The weather was bad and the flight became very rough, the plane occasionally dropping what seemed to be a thousand feet, but I suppose it was actually nearer to a hundred feet.

I'm ashamed to admit it, but when we were approaching Brownsville, I had promised myself, *If we ever reach the ground safely, I will hire a car to continue my journey.* And I breathed a sigh of relief when we touched down. All the passengers deplaned, as airport stops were longer in those days. During the stop I confronted myself: *Don't be a coward. Get back on that plane.* So, fearfully, I climbed aboard.

Soon a man sat down beside me. He said, "You are Dr. Norman Vincent Peale, aren't you? I have read your books. I understand we can expect a rough flight, and I'm a bit nervous. I decided if I could sit by Dr. Peale, I'd be fine. Hope you don't mind."

"Not at all," I said. But I thought, *Good thing he doesn't know what a slender reed he's leaning on!*

But I encouraged my seatmate, "Don't worry a bit. These planes are the 'workhorses' of the air transport industry. They bounce around some, but we'll get there safely. You can depend upon that." It was curious how having someone admittedly dependent upon me (and my assuming bravery I really did not feel) made the rough flight seem less so.

I think back with nostalgia to the many miles I flew on DC-3s. Nowadays I travel about 150,000 miles a year to speaking engagements, here and overseas.

One evening in 1936 I looked from our apartment window

at 25 Fifth Avenue and saw overhead a gigantic dirigible, serenely passing on its way to Lakehurst, New Jersey, to complete its transatlantic flight from Hamburg. It was the German airship *Hindenburg,* which on May 6, 1937, was to explode, its nose bursting into flames just as it approached the mooring mast. Thirty-five of the ninety-seven persons aboard and one man on the ground died. This disaster contributed to the end of dirigible travel.

On May 27, 1937, the great Golden Gate Bridge in San Francisco Bay was opened with two hundred thousand on hand to celebrate one of the engineering marvels of the century. It was heralded as the longest suspension bridge in the world, measuring 6,450 feet. At one point in the festivities, following music by several school girls' choirs, a man called, "Listen to the bridge!" The crowds were hushed and listened to an impressive symphony of sounds coming from the many wind-swept wires strung on the bridge.

In the thirties a movement known variously as totalitarianism, Nazism, or Fascism continued to develop in Europe, principally in Italy, Germany, and Spain.

In Spain it was led by Generalissimo Francisco Franco, in Italy by Benito Mussolini, and in Germany by Adolf Hitler. Fragmentary forms of this totalitarian movement existed to some extent elsewhere in Europe as well.

On August 7, 1936, a news dispatch from Washington described "Fascism, with its glorification of the state and its leader, its contempt for democracy and liberal institutions, its exaltation of the collective at the expense of the individual, its love of military display. . . . It is characterized by an official policy of anti-Semitism." The leaders arrogated to themselves positions of super glorification, Mussolini calling himself "Il Duce" and Hitler "Der Führer."

I recall being in Germany just after Hitler had come to

power. Everywhere in the country where two Germans met, they would stiffly give the Nazi salute, the right arm flung up, and greet each other with the words "Heil Hitler." I am proud that never once while I was in Germany did I give this Nazi salute, even out of courtesy—and that was long before it became widely recognized as despicable.

Once in preaching in our New York church to a capacity congregation, I was denouncing Nazism and Hitler when I noticed a man edging out of a pew in the rear of the auditorium. He had to squeeze past several people. In the aisle he faced the pulpit, clicked his heels together, gave me the Nazi salute, then whirled around and stamped out. I just went on telling of the abomination of Adolf Hitler.

By 1939 Hitler's army goose-stepped into Czechoslovakia and Poland. Hitler apparently thought he was on his way to mastery of the world. But he was mistaken, for looking ahead a short five years, a news bulletin (May 7, 1945) said, "Adolf Hitler is dead, his Reich, which he once exultantly claimed would live a thousand years, is destroyed, and the war in Europe is over."

It was late afternoon on September 2, 1936, when our second child came to join the family. John Stafford Peale was born at the French Hospital, a Catholic-owned-and-operated hospital on West Twenty-ninth Street in New York City.

We were pretty sure that sometime this day the baby would be born. I sat in Ruth's hospital room, biting my nails and assuring her that "everything was going to be fine," but I myself was more reassured by Ruth's calm and confident attitude. She always was a really positive thinker with strong faith.

Then the doctor, a good friend, came and said, "Norman, you can't do anything. Besides, it's getting along toward Sunday and you should be preparing your sermon. I suggest you go to your office. I'll let you know when the baby comes." Acknowledging my uselessness, I walked to my office in the church a few blocks away, praying all the way. About three hours later the doctor called. "You have a fine baby boy. You can come back now."

We had a summer seaside cottage, Cedar Crest, on Peconic Bay near Southampton, Long Island, and when Ruth was able to travel, we put baby John in a basket and drove about a hundred miles to Cedar Crest. Margaret, three years old, and Grandma Stafford welcomed the new arrival, and Margaret told us that she "would take charge of him."

From our children I have learned many things, and one lesson came about in this way. Both little children occupied the same room at 40 Fifth Avenue, where we were living at that time. We noticed that at an age when other children were talking, John seldom spoke, and this, of course, concerned us. I described this lack of speech to my great friend Dr. Smiley Blanton. He suggested that he come to our apartment and observe the children, which he did. After being in the room with them for a short time he came out and said, "It's very simple. Children are very smart. John realizes that his sister will talk for him, so he doesn't need to talk."

At the doctor's suggestion we installed John in his own room, and soon he was talking normally. Now he is a college professor, a Ph.D., no less, lecturing on philosophy.

The twentieth anniversary of the end of the First World War saw the birth or revival of a patriotic song called "God Bless America." It had been written for a musical in 1918 by Irving Berlin, and Kate Smith popularized it over radio on Armistice Day in 1938. It became a great success and still is sung with fervor all over the country.

I well remember the night in October 1938 when a radio program reported, with stark realism, an attack on earth by enormous figures from Mars. It was the night that Orson Welles and his players presented over the Columbia Broadcasting System "The War of the Worlds," based on a novel by H. G. Wells. With an audience of an estimated 6 million listeners, so realistic were the brutality, destruction, and death depicted that it created a national hysteria. I listened to this unforgettable broadcast, but, having heard previous announcements, I knew it was entirely theatrical. It proved, however, that national hysteria can quite easily be created.

The more realistic fear was of another world war. But the menacing war clouds were temporarily dispelled by a meeting in September of 1938 at Munich, attended by the "Big Four"— Adolf Hitler, British prime minister Chamberlain, French premier Daladier, and Italian dictator Mussolini. A reporter said, "It took the Big Four just five hours and twenty-five minutes at Munich to dispel the clouds of war and come to an agreement on the partition of Czechoslovakia. There was to be no European war after all."

Just six months later, German forces marched into Prague, and Czechoslovakia ceased to exist. Hitler had taken it over. Following Hitler's attack on Poland on September 3, 1939, Britain and France honored their treaty obligations to the Poles and declared war on Germany.

World War II had begun.

Meanwhile, here at home the depression continued. Despite the efforts of the federal government and American industry, the economy remained stagnant. The soup kitchen was an all-too-familiar sight. Many needy people were reduced to repeating the familiar words "Brother, can you spare a dime?" And as World War II erupted in Europe, the United States again tried to remain neutral as at the start of World War I.

Thus end the unforgettable thirties, to the sound of the roll of drums and marching feet, with FDR, like Wilson before him, trying to keep us out of war. Again, though, thousands of our men were to die before peace would come again.

But there was a personal end to the decade of the thirties that first shocked and then grieved me and finally deepened my faith. On the 28th of July, 1939, Ruth and I, with little Margaret and John, were at Father and Mother's home in Canisteo, New York, a beautiful pillared house on the hill. Though Mother was not well, we had a delightful family time together. Then Mother retired. Margaret and John were seated on her bed when I went in to say good-bye. I had to leave for New York to give my "Art of Living" radio program over NBC, and I said to Mother, "I love you and will see you on Monday."

But next morning Ruth called to convey the sad news that Mother had just died. I didn't at all expect this and had been encouraged by her liveliness the day before. Though it was Saturday and the offices at the church were closed, in a sense of shock and grief I went to the church and sat in the pulpit in the empty sanctuary, for Mother had said, "Whenever you go into the pulpit, I will be there with you." And I wanted to be with her.

I then went into my private office. On my desk was a Bible she had given me. I put my hands upon it, looking unseeingly out the big windows at Fifth Avenue. Then suddenly I felt two cupped hands on my head. It was the feel of her hands. I wept, although the touch deeply comforted me. Being of a practical, even scientific, turn of mind, I asked myself, *Can this be fantasy?* But it was definitely real, and I knew that if she could, she would return to comfort her son. And I believe that she did. Why was I given such a great spiritual experience? I do not know, but I do know that God is good.

CHAPTER 5

The Forties: Decade of War and Peace

THE fifth decade of this story was exciting. And *exciting* is the right word, for I cannot remember many dull moments—some hard times, but few dull ones.

In the census of 1940 the nation's population reached a new high, 131.6 million citizens. New York was the most populous state with 13.5 million people, Pennsylvania was second with 9.9 million, Illinois third with 7.7 million, Texas had 6.4 million, and California 5.1 million. Life expectancy had reached sixty-three years.

War clouds were increasing, and isolationists were urging the policy of "America first." A poll showed that more than a third of all Americans favored neutrality toward the war in Europe. But when France fell, the United States moved from a state of neutrality to one of nonbelligerency, edging ever nearer to a state of war.

President Roosevelt continued to express his hope that the U.S. would remain out of the war in Europe. He said, "We look forward to a world founded on four human freedoms: freedom of speech, freedom to worship God each in his own way, freedom from want, and freedom from fear." The president also proposed what was called the Lend Lease Program. It meant that billions of dollars worth of war matériel was to be given to Britain, the cost to be repaid in goods after the war. We would also allow British warships to be refueled and repaired in American naval yards.

On November 5, 1940, FDR broke the unwritten law of no third term for a President by defeating Wendell Willkie. However, the victory margin of the president was much less than in his first two elections, possibly because of the third-term issue. But Roosevelt's effort to lift the country out of the depression favorably influenced voters. John L. Lewis of the CIO union at first refused to support the president but finally did so on the ground that in war or the threat of war and in a grave depression "we should not change horses in the midst of a stream."

During this time of uncertainty about neutrality or entry into the war on the side of the Allies, I was busy with an ever-increasing congregation, many church activities, and a growing schedule of speeches. On speaking trips to the Midwest and West I noted that the farther I went from the eastern seaboard the less war talk was heard. Those areas were apparently too busy combating the effects of the depression and the Dust Bowl to be all that concerned about a war across the Atlantic Ocean.

But many people across the country were greatly interested in reports of advances made by CBS in color technology with an apparatus that transmitted color pictures by rotating color disks in front of a television camera. These early experiments now seem quite primitive, but then it was exciting in its possibilities. As it turned out, CBS's gamble did not pay off; an RCA color system won and was the basis for the ones we have in our TV sets today.

In 1940 Ernest Hemingway came out with his popular novel *For Whom the Bell Tolls.* For the first time in our history, FDR and Mackenzie King, the Canadian prime minister, agreed to establish a joint Board of Defense against possible attack by Germany. The Willys Corporation introduced a new vehicle nicknamed the "Jeep." The Mount Rushmore Memorial, carved by John Gutzon de la Mothe Borglum, featuring the faces of Washington, Lincoln, Jefferson, and Theodore Roosevelt, was completed in South Dakota. The Ford plant, heretofore nonunion, signed an agreement with the United Auto Workers Union. A National Gallery of Art was opened in Washington in March 1941. Funds were given by Andrew Mellon, former secretary of the treasury. The building displayed the Mellon collection and other works of art.

On December 27, 1940, as the first year of the decade came to a close, the president of the United States in a fireside chat warned that "America faces a perilous threat to its existence— not since Plymouth Rock and Jamestown has American civilization been in such danger as now." The president asserted that weapons of war would be sent to those nations that opposed Nazi Germany. Most Americans supported the president's policy of sending military supplies and old navy destroyers to Britain.

But that was not all of the war trouble facing the country. In October 1941 President Roosevelt had written Emperor Hirohito about the gravity of the situation between Japan and the United States. This had been accentuated by a U.S. embargo of oil to Japan and by the freezing of all Japanese assets in the U.S.

The Japanese cabinet had fallen, and a new cabinet, headed by Premier Tojo, had taken power. His cabinet was predominantly composed of military leaders, and Tojo himself was a general.

Then on Sunday, December 7, 1941, came Japan's sneak attack on Pearl Harbor, Hawaii. Japanese aircraft carriers approached within three hundred miles of Pearl Harbor and launched wave after wave of bombers. The surprise element was astounding. One independent radio operator got some blips indicating a massive movement somewhere but concluded it was our B-17 bombers being shifted from Wake Island to Pearl Harbor and did not report it. By 8:00 A.M. two U.S. battleships had been dealt fatal blows, and hundreds of American sailors had been killed. But our military soon got into action and drove off the invaders by 9:45 A.M. with a loss to the Japanese of twenty-nine aircraft.

The full news of this disaster was on radio that Sunday by noon in New York and aroused the city as seldom before. When I entered the pulpit for the Sunday evening service, the church was packed beyond capacity. The atmosphere was one of great tension. I realized the people wanted to express their feelings, so I said, "Folks, let us stand and sing 'The Star Spangled Banner.'" I've heard our national anthem in connection with various great events but never sung with such fervor as it was that night. The people knew that hundreds of American boys had given their lives for their country that day, and they thought of them as they sang. I sensed they were also singing their defiance of a ruthless military power.

After the national anthem I announced, "Now let's sing 'America,'" and "My country, 'tis of thee, sweet land of liberty" roared out, and people's eyes were blinded with tears. Then we offered a prayer for calmness and God's guidance. I also prayed for our Japanese fellow Christians. The depth of spiritual feeling equaled the surge of patriotism. It was a service that will never be forgotten by those who were present on that historic occasion.

The night after Pearl Harbor Sunday, a dinner of our Men's League was scheduled to be held in the church dining hall, and the speaker was to be Reverend Fojiro Shimuzu, pastor of the Japanese Reformed Church. Mr. Shimuzu telephoned me to cancel his engagement to speak "in view of the circumstances."

My reply was that the kingdom of God, of which we both were spiritual citizens, "was greater than any earthly kingdom," and I finally persuaded him to come and fulfill his engagement.

In introducing Mr. Shimuzu, I told of this telephone conversation and, as the speaker stood, the audience arose as one man. Everyone in that big crowd gave our Japanese Christian brother an ovation. With tears in his eyes, Mr. Shimuzu, who had long served God in this country, responded appropriately.

We had another good Japanese friend, Toro Matsumoto, who had been in the United States for some years and who spoke English fluently. He had graduated from seminary and desired ordination as a minister; he had been unanimously approved. The ordination service was scheduled to be held in our church three nights after Pearl Harbor Sunday. Some felt that, due to the high emotional reaction of the populace to the Japanese attack, the service should be delayed. But most of us felt the affairs of Christianity should not be determined by war hysteria, so we went ahead with the service. The police department circled the church with police protection during the service, but there was no trouble at all. Mr. Matsumoto went back to Japan after the war and became a very popular personality on radio, witnessing to his Christian faith.

Television in 1941 was not at all like that of today. On July 1 of that year commercial TV began with NBC and CBS offering competing programs. NBC was given a license for regular operation of station W2XBS for four hours of broadcasting a week, but NBC said it would be on the air for thirteen hours a week. CBS immediately matched it. However, only a few households had TV sets to receive the broadcasts from either company.

War and depression could be momentarily forgotten as sports fans enjoyed the athletic exploits of Joe DiMaggio, "Jolting Joe," as he was called. In the early weeks of the 1941 season, he hit safely in fifty-six consecutive games, finally bouncing into a double play with the bases loaded for his last ups in his fifty-seventh game. The Yankees won 4–3.

On December 8, 1941, President Roosevelt described December 7 as "a day which will live in infamy" and asked Congress to declare war against Japan. Six and a half minutes later, Congress complied. The vote in the Senate was unanimous, but one opposing vote was cast in the House of Representatives.

Germany and Italy immediately declared war on the United States. A big bright light over the entrance to the White House grounds was turned off. As two officials of the government noticed its absence, one asked, "I wonder how long it will be before that light is turned on again?"

"Until it is," said the other, "the lights will stay turned off over all the world."

The year 1942 opened with the battles of the Java Sea in the South Pacific, and Japan was admittedly the winner. Then came the fall of Bataan in the Philippines on April 9. An army of seventy-six thousand American soldiers was surrendered to the Japanese. General King, serving as commander under General Douglas MacArthur, said when he was compelled to surrender, "I feel like Robert E. Lee at Appomattox." Upon his departure for Australia, General MacArthur made his famous vow, "I shall return."

Things grew tougher for all Americans. On May 14, 1942, Americans lined up to receive their first ration books. Every family was limited to one pound of sugar every two weeks and gasoline was limited to twenty-five gallons per month. Butter became scarce, and darkened homes were the nightly rule.

After the fall of Corregidor and Bataan, the surrendered army of seventy-six thousand Americans was marched to prisoner-of-war camps. The Japanese had no respect for their prisoners because a Japanese soldier is expected to die before allowing himself to be taken prisoner. Therefore, the roads became lined with bayoneted prisoners, ruthlessly slain if they faltered or fell during the march. It was a sad day in America's history. All over the country, Americans toughed it out until victory ultimately came.

The better elements in all of our human nature are subordinated in the hatred and killing of war, and Americans as well as the Japanese and others have dark stains on war records. An example is the treatment of Japanese-Americans in this country during World War II. In the highly inflamed emotions of war, every person of Japanese name and features was suspected of being a potential enemy. But of the hundred thousand Japanese-Americans interned behind barbed wire and submitted to great indignities, two-thirds had been born in the United States and were, therefore, natural-born citizens of this country. More than ten thousand Americans of Japanese descent volunteered for combat in the war with Japan, and many became highly decorated heroes.

One night recently in New York City's Masonic Hall on Fourteenth Street, I had dinner with more than two thousand Masons and their spouses. I had the honor that night of sharing the speakers' platform with the famous General "Jimmy" Doolittle. As I listened to this great man, now over ninety years of age, modestly and in low-key fashion tell of his heroic raid over Tokyo in wartime, that American flyer, who is of less than average physical stature, struck me as possessing gigantic spirit and patriotism. With a squadron of B-25s he raided Tokyo, Osaka, Kobe, and Nagoya. Then all planes continued to China, where they landed on darkened airfields. They had taken off from carriers but at that time such large planes could not land on seagoing vessels, hence the China landing.

Meanwhile, war notwithstanding, the work of helping people went on. I recall vividly something that happened to one man in the 1940s that profoundly affected his subsequent life. This man came to the Blanton Peale Clinic for help. Dr. Blanton said he had one of the most hopeless cases of alcoholism he had ever worked with. Later he referred him to me with the statement, "This man is in your department, Norman. We have had him under treatment, to which he has only partially responded. At least he now understands himself, but the motivation necessary for a cure of the disease of alcoholism seems not to be strong enough to put him over the line to sobriety. He wants this to occur, but he does not want it enough to make it happen." I thought this was an expert analysis.

So I saw this patient. Let us call him Howard. I quoted Psalm 34, verse 6, to him. I knew he had been reared by a strong Bible-believing family down South and that he had a deep attachment to his parents and their Christian thinking. Verse 6 says, "This poor man cried, and the Lord heard him, and delivered him out of all his troubles."

"You see, Howard," I said, "the Lord does not do a halfway job. He goes all out; and if one has real faith, that person will be delivered of all his troubles, even a tough one like alcoholism. Tell you what I'll do. You are so weak that you need propping up, so I will have faith for you until you are able to go on your own." He seemed pleased and shook my hand with a firmer grip than before.

I recall distinctly that on the following Thursday afternoon about five o'clock, Howard came into my mind so strongly that I became concerned about him. And I sent up to God a strong prayer for Howard. I imagined Howard, wherever he was at that moment, experiencing God's care and help. I know it was five o'clock because my secretary had just said good night and left the office.

The following Sunday at church I was greeting a long line of people, and there was Howard. He said, "Doc, I've just gotta see you now."

He said this so intensely that I replied, "Go into my office. I'll see you there in a few moments when this line of folks ends."

As soon as I closed the office door, Howard said, "Doc, something strange happened to me last week. I can't figure it but . . . but . . . it was something powerful. I've gotta know what it is."

"Was it by any chance on Thursday?"

Surprised, he said, "Yes, it was Thursday about five o'clock." Then Howard told me the following story: "I was staying in the Parker House Hotel in Boston, and I'd had a tough day. When I entered the hotel, I passed the bar and the smell of alcohol coming out of there stopped me in my tracks. I wanted a drink like nobody's business. I just had to have only one drink.

"But something stopped me from going into that bar. I tried, thinking I would have just one little drink. But I knew it wouldn't be only one; I would come out on a binge. Then I saw a drugstore. I bought a pound box of candy, went to my room and ate it all. I sat there and cried like a baby and I said, 'OK, Jesus, I'm all Yours.' Then I felt peaceful."

I knew Howard until his death thirty years later, and alcohol was never again a problem for him. I've seen many demonstrations of power in my life. But what happened to this alcoholic ranks with the greatest power demonstration I've ever seen, alcoholism being what it is—such a strongly addictive disease.

In early spring of 1942 something else occurred that was one of the greatest surprises in my life. Sunday morning after church I was greeting people, when a lady said, "Congratulations."

"About what?" I asked, surprised.

"Don't you know?" she asked.

"No," I said.

She put her hands up to her mouth. "Oh, I've talked too much. I've spilled the beans. I've let the cat out of the bag. Please forgive me." And she scurried away in obvious discomfiture.

I was puzzled, but the incident went out of my mind until later Ruth and I were in the bedroom of our apartment, getting ready for lunch. The incident came back to me and I said, "Something strange happened to me this morning. You know Mrs. ———? Well, she congratulated me." Then I recounted the lady's strange behavior.

Ruth calmly said, "You have to know sometime. We are going to have another baby."

I was stunned. "Oh no," I said, sinking into a chair. (We still have that chair.) "Oh no," I repeated, "I can't go through that again."

Ruth, still calm, replied, "You won't have to. I will go through it. But don't you worry. I'll watch over you all the way."

Well, I survived, and on July 22, 1942, we awakened and Ruth said, "I have a feeling this is the day." So after breakfast she straightened the house, did a little ironing, then went to the beauty parlor so she would look her best at the hospital. I told her she looked OK to me. As for me, I spent the day trying to live up to my reputation as a positive thinker. In the afternoon she checked into the Olean, New York, hospital where my brother Robert Clifford Peale practiced medicine.

When the news came that Ruth's labor was accelerating, we were at dinner at Bob and Louise's home. Bob left for the hospital, saying, "You stay here. You can't do anything. You'll just be in the way." Thus put in my place for the third time, I finished my dinner. Louise was a wonderful cook. Finally, in the early evening Bob relented and had a nurse telephone to tell me I could come to the hospital to see my little daughter, our third child. When I saw Elizabeth Ruth Peale for the first time, she was holding up her little hand in the victory symbol, which at the time had been popularized by Winston Churchill—the first two fingers of the right hand forming a V for victory.

Elizabeth is now the wife of John M. Allen, formerly vice president of *Reader's Digest* and currently chairman of the board of the Foundation for Christian Living and vice president of *Guideposts* magazine.

According to a newspaper story back in 1942, a man who was termed "a relatively obscure officer" was appointed commander of the American forces in the European theatre. "He is Major General Dwight D. Eisenhower. The fifty-two-year-old Eisenhower, known as 'Ike,' was a football star at West Point, ranking 61 in a class of 164 at the military academy." But writing in 1990, we enthusiastically observe that student number sixty-one did pretty well subsequently in life.

Also, in June of 1942 the tide began to turn in the war. The American navy performed well by inflicting a crushing defeat on the Japanese in the battle of Midway. Our navy won this engagement, though faced by overwhelming odds in naval strength. On the European front German targets were bombed successfully by our inexperienced B-17 fleets, and U.S. soldiers won an important victory in the Solomon Islands. The Allies entered North Africa. For an unwarlike nation, the Americans were doing really well, carrying on two wars in widely separated sections of the world simultaneously. On January 24, 1943, Prime Minister Churchill and President Roosevelt, meeting in Casablanca, Morocco, announced that "the war will not end until the unconditional surrender of Japan, Germany, and Italy has been achieved," which indicates the positive spirit of the Allied leaders and supporting peoples.

The depth of sacrificial devotion to America's crusade for

freedom in the 1940s is poignantly illustrated by the heroic story of Commander Howard Gilmore. The powerful American submarine *Growler* ran into a Japanese gunboat at high speed and was riddled by machine gun fire. Many of the submarine crew were killed, and Commander Gilmore was mortally wounded. He might possibly have been saved, though bleeding profusely, if the crew of the *Growler* had delayed long enough to rescue him. But seeing that if the submarine lingered to try to rescue him it might be destroyed, Gilmore's last words were the command "Take her down!" His selfless action saved most of the crew and a prized submarine as well. Commander Gilmore was posthumously awarded the Medal of Honor.

So the war went on, the United States defeating the Japanese at Guadalcanal, and Major General George S. Patton, Jr., stopping the advance of the German commander Rommel at Tunisia in North Africa.

People at home valiantly did their part in achieving victory. A popular slogan those days was "Use it up, wear it out, make it do, or do without." They cheerfully endured such restrictions as four ounces of butter a week. Coffee and flour were rationed. Tuesdays and Fridays were meatless days. Men did without vests for their suits, and pants went without traditional cuffs. You could buy only three pairs of shoes a year. Rubber was inaccessible.

Delay was everywhere. Trains were late and crowded with soldiers. It was difficult to get a berth in a sleeping car. Workers were pampered with coffee breaks, unheard of before the war, but wages were frozen, as were salaries. U.S. war production industries produced as never before. The B-24 plant at Ford's Willow Run plant in Michigan produced planes at the rate of five hundred a month. Liberty ships were built one every four days, offsetting the heavy loss of shipping by German U-boat attacks. The staggering production of American industry even caused Stalin to speak admiringly. He said, "Without it the war would have been lost."

In October of 1943 the Allies successfully invaded Italy, and the Americans advanced on a wide front, eventually entering Rome triumphantly. Then came D day and the landing on the beaches of Normandy. The next year, General MacArthur came back to the Philippines as he had promised, saying, as he waded ashore, "People of the Philippines, I have returned." It was October 20, 1944. The Japanese lost Guam, and Premier Tojo's government fell, he who had instigated the attack on Pearl Harbor. Tojo, Mussolini, and Hitler were doomed as the 16 million Americans in uniform swept to victory.

All during the war I was busy on the home front where life went on. It had to go on. I was doing a lot of speaking before business conventions and sales rallies, trying to maintain the spirit of optimism and faith. But always I was back in New York City weekends to preach at the church. Often I would leave by sleeper train Sunday night and on Monday night would be speaking in some city or town perhaps a thousand miles away. I traveled mostly by train in those days, at first in single berth Pullmans. Then they invented the Pullman bedroom, a small room with lower and upper berth. Mirror and wash basin could be pulled out of a wall above a toilet, which doubled as an upholstered seat. The room was a comfortable accommodation by night or day.

I wrote some of my forty books in train bedrooms. Perhaps a book about some bizarre travel experiences I've had in connection with speaking engagements might be interesting. Also I've threatened to write a book on "Hotels I've Stayed In." But generally hotels and motels today are uniformly better than they were years ago, though prices, of course, are much higher. I remember the sense of extravagance I had one night many years ago, checking into the Mark Hopkins Hotel in San

Francisco and seeing on the slip that the rate was twenty dollars. Today if a check-in slip quoted that little figure, I would frame it.

The growth of television is evidenced by a Gallup poll taken in 1945, which showed that 81 percent of the American people had never seen a television set in operation. I personally remember both my first radio program, heard in 1923, involving a church service at Mathewson Street Methodist Church in Providence, Rhode Island, and my first TV show, coming from a studio in New York City to Pawling, New York, in 1947.

I've had many interesting and sometimes inspiring experiences on speaking trips. One night, for example, after speaking in the City Center in Oklahoma City, I returned to my hotel and the phone rang. It proved to be the quiet, cultured voice of a lady who informed me that a prayer meeting was going on at her home. She said, "I am sure you have never been in a prayer meeting like this one. I'm sending a couple of dry alcoholics to bring you here."

"But, ma'am," I said, "I am leaving in the morning on a very early plane. Please excuse me. But thank you for inviting me. Have them pray for me."

Just then came a rap at my door and two young men explained, "We are the dry alcoholics Mrs. ——— sent to take you to the prayer meeting." So I gave in and went with them to a suburban neighborhood. The living room was crowded with no fewer than fifty people, sitting on anything suitable. One young woman was even perched on the grand piano. A great shout went up as we entered, and the crowd burst into a song that someone explained was their welcome song. It was anything but a gathering of "pious" people, though they were all believers, no doubt about that.

Somebody gave me a chair, saying, "We always give a chair to a guest. Next time you sit where you can." Then spontaneous prayers continued: prayers of thanksgiving or intercession for anyone who was sick or had a problem. Most prayers were giving thanks for blessings. Some prayed for those who had not yet had a Christian experience.

Finally they turned to witnessing about what their faith had accomplished. Someone would start a hymn and all joined in. One young woman, with braces on both legs, said, "I was told I would never walk again. But God led me to a doctor who told me that my faith and God's guidance might heal me. See me walk." She walked with some awkwardness, but she walked.

A young man witnessed, "I was fired from three jobs. Then I found Jesus, who straightened me out. I am now in middle management and really organized. I see super possibilities in my future."

The meeting concluded about one o'clock in the morning with everyone holding hands and forming a circle. Then a chain of short prayers ran around the circle, giving me the feeling that I had hold of something like an electric wire. There was power in that circle of praying people, every one of them really believing and turned on.

In connection with my church in New York City, it required a long time, years, in fact, to overcome the empty pews and the sense of failure that prevailed when we came in 1932. But beginning in the late thirties, continuing all through the forties, fifties, and until now, the church has been crowded with people every Sunday.

The depression was still hanging on in the early forties and did not really end until World War II created wartime prosperity. But depression of mind and spirit is more complex and did not abate until much later. Indeed, that form of depression seems perennial. But in the 1940s it was more acute.

I have always given encouraging messages, either in spoken or written form, for in my opinion Christianity teaches that with God's help we can endure, we can overcome. We can find a better way, a better life.

People sensed that positive and hopeful messages were given in our church, for they began to come and continued to come to listen, not to a scholarly, theological sermon, but to a simple, sincere message by a humble, plainspoken believer who loves people and who wanted to help them to a better, happier, more fulfilled life.

Soon many were asking for printed copies of the talks. Since the spoken messages were always given ad lib, totally without a manuscript, reproduction became a problem. But we believe every problem can be solved. And we solved that problem by having the sermon taped, typed up, mimeographed, then mailed to whoever requested them.

In time these requests became so numerous that we needed a building with the equipment for direct mail. Ruth and I, having purchased a country home in the rural section of the town of Pawling, Dutchess County, New York, erected our building in that village, on Route 22. It has been added to many times and now contains more than seventy-five thousand square feet and employs 125 people, mailing Christian messages to a million people with a readership of 5 million. The nonprofit organization is called the Foundation for Christian Living. Ruth is the head of this activity, assisted by young and deeply committed executives and personnel.

About five years after the Foundation for Christian Living was founded in 1940, in the early fall of 1945 Raymond Thornburg, a neighbor in Pawling, along with Ruth and me, got another brilliant and creative idea. We should start a new magazine and in it print the stories of people who had been turned on to dynamic and positive faith and who had had exciting things happen to them as a result. Ruth and I had already been thinking along those lines, when it happened that our old friends Raymond and Pherbia Thornburg came to us with a spiritual letter service idea. It seemed we could merge the two concepts, and we did so.

We had no money to establish a magazine of national circulation, but Ruth said, "This country needs a publication in which exciting, even thrilling stories of God working in people's lives may be told." Somehow we collected from friends about seventy-five hundred dollars, the smallest amount, probably, with which a national circulation magazine was ever established. Starting in pamphlet form, it soon became a small, easily handled magazine and continues in that popular size.

We called it *Guideposts*, meaning the way to a happy and victorious life-style and the way to true success and fulfillment in life. Now, forty-five years later, *Guideposts* has the twelfth largest circulation among all magazines published in the United States. It takes no advertising and circulates to subscribers only. Its business office is in Carmel, New York, and its editorial offices at 747 Third Avenue, New York City. It publishes monthly the most exciting, inspiring, motivational, true stories about how people of faith and positive thinking turn back failure, overcome hazards and difficulties, and achieve goals, living very creative and fulfilled lives.

On April 12, 1945, President Roosevelt died suddenly at Warm Springs, Georgia, and Vice President Harry S. Truman became the thirty-third president of the United States. I knew Harry Truman quite well. For some reason he once told a reporter that "Dr. Peale is a real man." I never knew what he had in mind in saying that, except that he once told me, "I like people like you, with spunk." You will pardon me for mentioning this, as I figure it was an extraordinary compliment, considering the source.

If I may say so, he was a real man himself, and he had that "spunk" to which he referred. This reminds me of a story

Governor A. Harry Moore, four-term governor of New Jersey, once told me about his mother, a spunky Christian widow who raised her son in very straitened circumstances.

Harry came home from school one afternoon, threw his cap at the old-fashioned hat rack in the corner of the kitchen, which served also as living room, and slumped into a chair. "What's troubling you, Son?" his mother asked.

"Oh, I can never amount to anything. We're poor, no pull, no opportunity."

Mama Moore was stirring something in a big pot on the coal stove. She pointed the big spoon at her boy, drops falling unheeded to the floor. "Never let me hear you talk like that, Son. We're people of faith. What you need is God and gumption."

What is gumption? It is an old word and means never give up, have faith, common sense, guts, character . . . you name it!

Truman inherited the war, and to end it he made some tough decisions. One was to bomb Hiroshima and Nagasaki. That must have been an agonizing decision. I didn't agree with all of his decisions—for instance, when he fired MacArthur—but I admired his ruggedness. And he was a believer, too, as all our Presidents have been whom I have known, each in his own way. And I've had the honor to have met them all, starting with Theodore Roosevelt.

I had the interesting experience of two meetings with General Douglas MacArthur, supreme commander in the Japanese war, who took their surrender on the battleship *Missouri* and became the virtual ruler of defeated Japan, serving in that capacity with compassion and wisdom. He said that he always believed in victory and never accepted a defeat as final. He lived that attitude.

I have headed this chapter of our nine-decade story "Decade of War and Peace." And peace finally came on a beautiful day in the summer of 1945. We were at our country home at Pawling when suddenly the bell in Christ Church on Quaker Hill began ringing. It kept on ringing until all the people on the hill knew it was calling everyone to come to the church for an important, historic meeting. People came in the casual clothes they happened to be wearing on a summer day in the country. The church was filled to its capacity, some standing. Among them were the parents of boys not yet home and a few who would never come home.

The minister came to me where I was seated toward the back. He is my longtime and good friend, Dr. Ralph Lankler. He said, "We must have a speech and we want you to do it."

I replied, "Ralph, you are the minister. You should speak to your congregation."

"No, I will conduct the service."

Then I saw Governor Thomas E. Dewey and Lowell Thomas in the crowd.

"Ralph, the governor is the natural speaker for an historic occasion, the end of a great war. Go and ask Tom or Lowell."

He did so, but he was soon back. "They said this is a deeply spiritual occasion—boys have died for God, country, and freedom. They both want you to speak." I was not dressed for the pulpit, with no tie and a sport jacket, but I went up and tried to speak to the people about our country—that they should love and serve it in life as those who died loved it and gave their lives.

Then I said, "We have two great Americans in our midst, our great governor, Tom Dewey, and that famous American, Lowell Thomas, as well as Ralph, our minister, and I do not think this occasion would be complete without a word from each of them."

None of them was dressed for the occasion either, but they came forward and each said a few inspiring words. I shall always remember this service on the day the great war ended. It seemed so appropriate to be called by the bell to the church on the hill, reminding us of God and country and of our duty to love and serve each.

The 1940s can truly be called the unforgettable decade of war and peace.

CHAPTER 6

The Fifties: Decade of Advance

THE second great war was over. The depression was ended. The psychology of the decade was to go forward in a time of peace, of progress, and of unlimited opportunity.

As the war came to an end, two super powers dominated the world: the United States of America and the Soviet Union. According to calculations made immediately after the war, Russia had suffered the loss of more than 6 million soldiers killed. The Japanese surrender marked the end of a five-year period that had no precedent and could be compared only to the Black Death in the fourteenth century, when one-third of the population of Europe died. Not since that time had so many people been killed as in World War II. Nor had so many of the living had their lives so uprooted, so changed and altered.

Germany and Italy were prostrate. The British suffered acutely. London had acres of appalling ruin. Japan appeared to be completely ruined. That appraisal made in 1945 is difficult to realize today when Japan seems to be reaching for the business leadership of the world. London has been thoroughly restored, and Italy is thriving. Germany has just achieved the unification of its separated West and East areas. This will mean a restoration of the old Germany in form, though we hope not in militaristic spirit.

America came out of the war better than any other nation, but of the 16 million Americans in uniform, four hundred thousand were killed, and more than five hundred thousand suffered wounds that in many cases affected their lives thereafter. One wonders how many great leaders were lost—how many gifted writers, musicians, inventors, business geniuses. We will never know. But no bomb damage was suffered by the United States, except on the day Japan attacked Pearl Harbor. There were assets, however, if the word can appropriately be used, because many medical advances were made, thousands of industries developed, the economy surged, and America developed the highest standard of living in the world.

As General MacArthur put down his pen after affixing his signature to the surrender documents aboard the battleship *Missouri*, he made a significant statement that people everywhere appreciated, particularly in the United States. He said, "Now men everywhere can walk upright in the sunlight." So the decade of the fifties was one of advance.

The 1950s were, in many respects, the best years in terms of attendance at religious services and respect for the opinions of religious leaders. Inspirational books by such popular figures as Bishop Fulton J. Sheen and Dr. Billy Graham became best-sellers, and it was in the fifties that my book *The Power of Positive Thinking* was published. Indeed, religion in the nation was at a high peak in its influence.

I have been with Billy Graham on several occasions. I sat with him on the platform at the Madison Square Garden on one of the nights of the New York Crusade during the fifties. The Garden was packed to capacity, with people standing, and hundreds outside who could not get into the great auditorium.

Observing all this, I turned and said to Billy, "Billy, how in the world do you do this?"

He turned to me with a grin and said, "Positive thinking, Norman—just the practice of positive thinking."

I regard Billy Graham as the greatest clergyman of his time. He has reached more people with the gospel than any other man alive, but none of the adulation has ever changed him from being Billy Graham, a humble disciple of Jesus Christ.

One day I called to see his mother in Charlotte, North Carolina, toward the end of her life. I had met her several times previously, and, being in the city on a speaking engagement, I wanted to pay my respects. I sat with her in her home, and naturally the conversation turned to Billy. She said, "I am very proud of him. He loves the Lord and loves to lead people to Him." Then she added quietly, "He is a good boy. Always has been a good boy."

On two occasions Billy and I have stayed at the same hotel in Switzerland, and I joined in meetings with the clergy in those cities, Montreaux and Lucerne.

Although World War II was over, the world was not entirely free of war.

The decade was only six months old when President Truman authorized General Douglas MacArthur, commanding general of American Far East forces, to provide the Republic of Korea troops with American naval and air power. The American government and the United Nations took a firm stand against Communist aggression from North Korea. The war dragged on, with the Chinese Communists helping the North Koreans, always threatening to enter in full force.

Some happenings that had nothing to do with war are interesting. Frank MacNamara, the head of a small finance firm, ran up a formidable restaurant bill in entertaining guests. When the bill was presented to him, he found that he hadn't the cash to pay it. Vowing such an embarrassment would never happen again, he invented a "Diner's Club" credit card. At the start it was carried by some two hundred people and had twenty-eight participating establishments. Thus began the credit card industry, which has now made cash almost irrelevant.

Charles Schultz came out with his now famous cartoon "Peanuts." It was rejected by many syndicates at first. But "Charlie Brown" was a positive thinker, taking every defeat philosophically, until he finally caught on. The census taken in 1950 showed the American population at 150.6 million people. Rural or farm dwellers had declined to 5.4 million, while urban population had risen to 64 percent of the total. The number of unemployed had declined to fewer than 2 million. The average weekly wage had hit a new high of $60.53.

One of the most controversial events of President Truman's administration took place when the president relieved General MacArthur of command on April 11, 1951, for insubordination. Subsequently, the general made his famous speech to both houses of Congress, concluding with the memorable phrase, "Old soldiers never die; they just fade away." I recall joining the multitudes on Fifth Avenue cheering MacArthur as he rode in parade through the city on April 20, 1951.

At this time, millions of devoted fans of Lucille Ball, then Lucy Arnaz, were watching and thoroughly enjoying her half-hour television show "I Love Lucy." I knew Lucy as a close friend. A firm Christian believer, she often attended my church services. Ruth and I were at her home in Palm Springs one night for dinner when the local priest called on the telephone. A maid handed the message to Lucy, who answered in character. "Tell the good Father that I'll call him in the morning. This is Protestant night." At one time Lucy had guests on TV, and

I was privileged to be one of them. It was a rollicking, happy show. She was a great performer, a great woman, a great American.

Lucy came from Jamestown, New York. Though she lived in California most of her life, she apparently had a nostalgia for the scenes of her childhood. She would often say to Ruth and me in the spring, "I always miss the lilacs in the month of May."

I always made it a policy to counsel a couple about to be married, and I recall that I had Lucy and Gary Morton in my study at the church before their wedding. I said to the bride-groom, "Gary, you know that Lucy becomes volatile at times and may, as the saying goes, 'hit the ceiling.' What will you do?"

Gary quietly said, "Oh, I'll just wait until she comes back down." I knew then that it would be a good marriage.

It was a privilege to have the friendship of Lucy. She was a rarely gifted lady and good all the way through her wonderful personality. Gary Morton, her husband for many years, and my good friend, called me during her last illness. And I prayed for her daily.

Another TV show that achieved great success and popularity in the fifties was "The Roy Rogers Show." By then 3.8 million households had TV sets, or 9 percent of all the homes in the country, and this number was growing rapidly. Color TV was in its infancy but was fast being perfected. In addition to the "I Love Lucy" program and "The Roy Rogers Show," Imogene Coca and Sid Caesar were also popular with the ever-increasing number of TV viewers.

Ruth and I have been honored for years by friendship with Roy Rogers and Dale Evans, two of the warmest performers ever to be taken to the hearts of all Americans. They personified the old West, riding their horses and singing their famous song "Happy Trails to You." They are also two of the most dedicated, loyal Christians I have known in my life. Whenever they were performing at Madison Square Garden, they invariably were in church every Sunday, and I happen to know that they live their faith every day.

One time when I was preaching for my friend Dr. Robert Schuller in the great Crystal Cathedral in Garden Grove, California, he also had Roy and Dale on the program. Roy stood before the congregation of thousands, looked around at the big church, and said, "My, but this place would hold a lot of hay." The huge congregation roared, then were led to the verge of tears as they heard these two favorites sing their famous duet, "Happy Trails." The big crowd stood in an ovation to two of the best people I've ever known.

Another show business personality I have had the pleasure of knowing is Bob Hope, a great citizen of the twentieth century. Besides the superlative art of helping people by laughter, Bob Hope is also a highly constructive leader of our time. I once wrote him, asking if he would contribute to our feature "Great Moments in Positive Thinking" in our magazine *PLUS*. He wrote me the following paragraphs, so characteristically Bob Hope:

> *I was standing in front of the Woods Theatre Building on Randolph Street in Chicago in 1928. I couldn't get a job. Across the street was a restaurant called Henrici's. It had a big open window, and you could see people eating. I wasn't eating too well at that time, but I had a lot of confidence that something would happen to get me a better menu.*
>
> *Along came a friend of mine and asked me how I was doing. "I'm starving," I replied.*
>
> *"Come with me," he said. He took me upstairs in the Woods Theatre Building and introduced me to a wonderful agent, who gave me a job for one day. After seeing my act, he gave me a job in a motion-picture house in a band show. I was emcee there for six months and have never stopped working since.*
>
> *The positive influence was that I stuck it out and was al-*

most sure that something had to happen. And, regardless of my shortened menu, it did. What I'm trying to say is, if you have a thought and you think it's a good one, stay with it.

On September 8, 1951, full sovereign rights were restored to Japan by the United States and forty-seven other nations. The steamship *United States*, the largest passenger ship to carry the American flag, was "floated out" at Newport News, Virginia, on June 23, 1951. She was only forty feet shorter than the *Queen Elizabeth*. In July of 1952 the Republican Convention in Chicago nominated Dwight D. Eisenhower and Richard M. Nixon for president and vice president, and the Democratic Convention, also meeting in Chicago two weeks later, chose as their candidates Governor Adlai E. Stevenson of Illinois for president and Senator John J. Sparkman of Alabama for vice president.

Eisenhower and Nixon were elected on November 4, 1952, by a landslide that carried with them both houses of Congress, and General Eisenhower became the thirty-fourth president of the United States.

Eisenhower was the first president whose inauguration was shown on television. At noon on January 20, 1953, he was seen taking the oath of office with Vice President Nixon and other notables looking on. Prior to this date, Mr. Eisenhower, as president-elect, had fulfilled a promise made in the campaign to visit the American troops in Korea. There he appeared in his old army uniform and promised to continue the struggle against Communism.

The year 1952 was quite important in my own life, for on October 13 Prentice Hall published my book *The Power of Positive Thinking*. This date of publication, October 13, was set because the publisher's birthday was on October 13 and the Prentice Hall Publishing Company was founded on October

13. Therefore, the thirteenth was considered a lucky day to launch a book. And while I have doubts about luck in general, I must say that contrary to all my expectations, the book proved very successful, for it has now sold 20 million copies worldwide. Actually, "it became one of the most successful books ever published," to quote a researcher.

After I had been on Ralph Edwards famed TV show "This Is Your Life," one of the most popular TV shows of the era, *The Power of Positive Thinking* surged to the number one position on best-seller lists all over the country. It was number one on the *New York Times* best seller list for 186 weeks and now, thirty-nine years later, is still selling well.

Then the trouble began. I was attacked for a book that was written in "simple language." Critics also condemned it as a "get ahead, get rich" manual, and a Methodist bishop condemned it as a "perversion" of Christianity. A few professors in colleges said less than complimentary things about it. I remember a remark by Stanley High, one of the editors of *Reader's Digest*, an acknowledged scholar. "Norman, if you made your simplicities sufficiently complex so that you could not be understood, they would leave you alone, and," he added laughingly, "so would the book buyers."

I was dumbfounded by the untruths critics repeated. The book was intended to, and did, support Christianity. Indeed, I received scores, even hundreds, of letters saying, "Your book sent me to the Bible, and the Bible turned my life around." Because of the attacks upon me, I thought for a time of leaving the church, but I realized there were thousands of fair-minded, kindly people in the church. In addition, I learned something important to anyone on how to deal with criticism: consider it seriously; if it is valid, learn from it; if it is not valid, forget it; and love the critics. This attitude toward criticism greatly strengthened me and, in time, worked a strange magic as illustrated by a conversation between Dr. Arthur Caliandro, my successor at the New York church where I had been senior minister for fifty-two years, and Cynthia Wedel, president of the National Council of Churches. Cynthia asked Arthur, "How is Norman?"

Arthur replied, "He is fine. He has outlived all his critics."

"Oh no," Cynthia replied, "he has outloved them."

Indeed I discovered a vital truth about living: loving your enemies is the greatest "weapon" in unfair attacks on oneself. Anyway, now in 1990, as I write this book, *The Power of Positive Thinking* has been translated into forty-four languages and is still having a steady sale.

Not only did I learn how to take criticism, but I also learned that if you feel something deeply, don't let even your friends discourage you. Always stick with your deepest feelings. For example, after I had written *The Power of Positive Thinking*, I showed the manuscript to a publisher, a friend of mine. He read it and said, "This won't sell at all." Then he added, "Better retitle it 'How to Live 24 Hours a Day.'"

So what did I do? I cut the manuscript up, putting the pieces in boxes labeled from 1 to 24. But soon I saw that this plan would not work and chucked the whole project. It lay dormant for a year on a closet shelf in our farmhouse in the country. Then Ruth, my wife, who always believed in the book, took an exact copy of the manuscript to Myron Boardman, president of the Trade Book Division of Prentice Hall, Inc., who said, "This book will be a best-seller if you change the title from *The Power of Faith* to a phrase you have in the manuscript that says the same thing more effectively: *The Power of Positive Thinking*." Ruth agreed immediately to the change, I more reluctantly.

But I was wrong, for the changed title worked its way into the English language and even into world culture through many languages. I believe God, who works in human affairs, gave me that title to cause many to embrace faith. Why did He give it to me of all people? I don't know. I've noticed that He chooses the most unlikely people to serve His purposes. We have had the title and the phrase *The Power of Positive Thinking* meticulously researched, and it has never been used before— the idea, yes, but the phrase, no. This fact has evidenced to me, at least, that God does indeed work mysteriously, His wonders to perform.

God was working in other people, too, as He is today. In earlier years in this century there was a dread disease called poliomyelitis, or "infantile paralysis," which particularly struck children, killing or crippling them. I had three young children, so I was deeply concerned, as were parents everywhere. But God was working through a man named Jonas Salk, of the University of Pittsburgh. He was a brilliant scientist who dis-covered with his colleagues that infantile paralysis was caused by three viruses. Dr. Salk tested four hundred thousand children with three vaccines and they proved to be safe and 70 percent effective. The government licensed the vaccine on April 12, 1954, two hours after the results of his testing was reported. Thus Dr. Jonas Salk, with his colleagues, became one of the great benefactors of humanity. I have the faith to believe that in the fullness of time, the same victory will come in the battle against cancer.

In 1954 General Electric hired an actor to host its television anthology series, "The General Electric Theatre," and to tour its plants to speak on the virtues of free enterprise and the American way. The actor's name: Ronald Reagan.

Social advance was given impetus by the Supreme Court when it struck down the "separate but equal" policy. This long-standing policy, which had permitted the segregation of public schools racially, was reversed on May 17, 1954, when in a unanimous decision of the Supreme Court it was declared unconstitutional.

In 1955 the United States sent military advisers to Vietnam in view of the Communist threat. Events to come were beginning to throw their shadows.

President Eisenhower signed a bill on June 14, 1954, that inserted the words "under God" into the Pledge of Allegiance. At the signing, "Ike" said, "These words will serve to rededicate the nation to its Divine Source and will tend to counter violence and a materialistic philosophy of life which deadens millions."

I came to know President Eisenhower quite well. On one occasion I was on the platform with him at Charlotte, North Carolina. Governor Luther Hodges, a close friend of mine, had asked me to give the prayer on an important state occasion when the president was to speak. As I stood at the podium and started to offer the prayer, I sensed that someone was standing slightly behind me. I looked quickly and it was the president, with his head bowed and eyes closed. He had stepped forward from his seat to stand with me, and I felt his support of prayer to God.

Later I was asked to a picnic where everyone sat on the grass behind the speakers' platform, and we all ate sweet corn on the cob. I noticed that Ike ate two ears. One reason everyone "liked Ike" was that, to the end, he was a grown-up American boy.

Several times I accepted the invitation of J. Edgar Hoover, director of the FBI, to speak at the commencement exercises of the FBI Police Academy in Washington. Each time they graduated many hundreds of police chiefs and other officers. On the first of these engagements, I was shown to a chair near the director, but there was a vacant chair between us. Soon President Eisenhower entered and took that chair. He said to me, "Give us a talk on positive thinking. I need it and so do all these police officers." I proceeded to speak in my usual energetic style, and when I sat down after completing my talk, the president said, "I like that. I always like a speaker who fights bees."

Then the director handed out diplomas one by one, during which time Ike talked to me. He leaned over my way, crossing his legs in such a manner that his bare leg showed. He was wearing old-fashioned garters and a nervy photographer snapped a picture, which appeared in a Washington paper. They gave me a copy and Ike autographed it. It hangs in my office today.

I asked him that day who was the greatest among all the great men he knew? He answered, "The greatest person I have ever known wasn't a man. It was a woman, my mother." He described her as a saintly lady and smart, too. "Often in this job [being president] I have wished I could consult her about questions, particularly about people. But she is in heaven. However, I knew her mind so well that many times I have felt I knew what she would say."

Then he told me this story. One night in their farm home Mrs. Eisenhower was playing a card game with her boys. "Now don't get me wrong," said Ike. "It was not with those cards that have kings, queens, jacks, and spades on them. Mother was too straitlaced for that." I seem to remember that President Eisenhower said the game they were playing was called Flinch. "Anyway, Mother was the dealer, and she dealt me a very bad hand. I began to complain. Mother said, 'Boys, put down your cards. I want to say something, particularly to Dwight. You are in a game in your home with your mother and brothers who love you. But out in the world you will be dealt bad hands without love. Here is some advice for you boys. Take those bad hands without complaining and play them out. Ask God to help you, and you will win the important game called life.'" And the president added, "I've tried to follow that wise advice always."

My friend Virgil Pinkley, in his book *Eisenhower Declassified,* tells of Billy Graham calling to see Ike in his last illness. When Dr. Graham started to leave, the general asked in a firm, strong voice, "Billy, can an old sinner like me ever go to heaven?"

"Of course, General Ike. You have made the ultimate decision—the greatest single decision that anyone can make. You have accepted Jesus Christ as your Savior; you have asked forgiveness for your sins. Of course you will go to heaven."

As Billy Graham was closing the door, he looked back. Tears were streaming down the face of Dwight D. Eisenhower, who had lived, loved, and fought as a true Christian.

We have called the fifties "the decade of advance." And it was that for our black citizens. One step of their advance was achieved on November 13, 1956, when the Supreme Court ruled segregation on buses to be unconstitutional. It was another victory of the nonviolent policy advocated by Martin Luther King, Jr., who said, "Nonviolence is the most potent technique for oppressed people."

On November 6 in the presidential election Dwight D. Eisenhower scored a landslide victory over Adlai E. Stevenson, carrying with him back into office for another term the forty-three-year-old vice president Richard Nixon. Ike was sixty-six years of age.

As we approached the end of the decade of the 1950s, we who had lived in the horse-and-buggy days of 1900 and 1910 and who went to the West Coast by train, traveling days to reach our destination (without diners, stopping at the Harvey restaurants while the conductor held his watch impatiently), could scarcely believe that American Airlines could announce same-day passenger service from East to West and West to East on its Boeing 707 jet aircraft. So the route that took weeks by prairie schooner and days by slow, non-air-conditioned trains was now five hours by airplane. America has grown up on miracles. Perhaps it ought to be called "The Miracle Country."

Alaska became the forty-ninth state on January 3, 1959. It was also hailed as the nation's largest state in land area (more than twice the size of second-largest Texas) but the least populous. Hawaii was proclaimed the fiftieth state by President Eisenhower on August 21, 1959. These were the first new states to achieve statehood since President Taft made Arizona a state in 1912.

The vice president in both terms of the Eisenhower administration was Richard M. Nixon, whom I came to know very well. Often called one of the best brains we ever had in public service, he was also quite intrepid, as evidenced during his trip to Latin America in 1958. Nixon encountered violence in Lima, Peru. He had been scheduled to meet a student group at the University of San Marco. On arrival at the university, he was confronted by a big crowd of hostile demonstrators. Against the advice of security, he climbed out of the car and plunged into the mob.

He was hit by a stone, shoved, and spat upon. By his sheer courage he won the admiration of people everywhere. When Vice President and Mrs. Nixon returned to Washington, they were warmly cheered by vast crowds. He said later that Latin America supports the United States, that "minority elements of Communists were responsible for the disturbance."

After Nixon was nominated for vice president, he came to my church the following Sunday, and I said, "Senator Nixon, it is an honor to meet you."

"Oh," he replied, "you have met me many times." He explained that during the war he was a junior naval officer stationed in New York. "Pat and I came to your church every Sunday and always shook hands with you afterward." I smiled somewhat sheepishly.

On one occasion I was invited to speak to congressional secretaries at a luncheon in the capitol building in Washington.

I was surprised to see Vice President Nixon in the audience. Afterwards I walked with him to his office, at which time he asked me how I prepared speeches and about my manner of delivery. "Mr. Vice President," I said, "it is astonishing that you, the vice president of the United States, who are an accomplished and terrific speaker, should ask me about making a speech!"

Mr. Nixon said, "I am always learning from people."

I was impressed with his humility and insatiable desire to improve.

Nikita Khrushchev, the Russian premier, toured the United States and at the United Nations showed his disrespect by taking off his shoe and using it to bang on his desk during his diatribe. I attended a luncheon where the Russian premier was to speak and sat beside Walter Hoving, the head of Tiffany's, one of New York's famous stores. We watched Khrushchev as he removed his shoe again and placed it on the table. The band struck up *The Star Spangled Banner*, and everyone in the huge crowd sprang to his feet and sang with extraordinary spirit. As we sat down, Walter Hoving said, "The way this crowd sang sure tells Khrushchev something." He didn't bang his shoe again.

Richard Nixon encountered the premier in Moscow, where he opened a U.S. National Exhibition and talked with him at the display of a model kitchen. Khrushchev challenged him, and the heated exchange that developed became known as the "kitchen debate." The Russian asserted that women in his country had modern conveniences too. But the fact was that they were not comparable to those in American households.

In 1956 Premier Khrushchev offered a chilling threat to Western diplomats: "Whether you like it or not, history is on our side. We will bury you." That is probably what the Communists thought was a likely outcome. But history has already buried Khrushchev. Now the shoe is on the other foot, and more than seventy years after the Russian Revolution of 1917, Communism has turned out to be a complete flop.

As a baseball fan I joined with all New York and Brooklyn fans of the Giants and the Dodgers in their grief and protests when those two teams moved in 1958, the Giants to San Francisco and the Dodgers to Los Angeles. But the Yankees and the Mets have very well preserved championship teams for New York.

Carl Erskine, a great pitcher and my longtime friend, pitched the first major league game played in Los Angeles on opening day against the Giants, and Carl won that game.

Carl was signed by Branch Rickey in 1948 for the then Brooklyn Dodgers and brought up to the big leagues from Fort Worth of the Texas League. Branch Rickey, whom I knew well, was very proud of Carl Erskine, calling him one of the greatest pitchers of that era. Carl's pitching record bears out this appraisal.

The following incident of a World Series game in 1952 may illustrate how Erskine had more than pitching control. He had what it took to control a crisis situation.

The Dodgers were battling the Yankees in what the media called "the Subway World Series." It was the fifth game of the series and Carl was behind, 5–4. In that fifth inning the Yankees reached Carl and took the lead away from him.

In the hubbub that ensued, Carl saw his manager, Charley Dressen, coming to the mound. Dressen took the ball from Carl's hand, and Erskine fully expected to be taken out. "How do you feel?" Dressen asked.

"Well, they have given me a tough time, but I feel fine."

Dressen then asked, "Carl, isn't today your wedding anniversary?"

Carl replied, "Yes, it's our fifth anniversary."

"Is Betty here and are you taking her out to celebrate tonight?"

"Well, yes," stammered Carl.

Ruth and I with Margaret, Elizabeth, and John.

With President Herbert Hoover.

A meeting with President Harry Truman, and other religious leaders.

I am seated beside President Dwight D. Eisenhower at the commencement exercises of the FBI Police Academy in Washington. This is the famous "garter picture."

LEFT: *With Major General Ormond R. Simpson, commanding general of the First Marine Division, after I spoke at the Seventh Marines Memorial Service on Hill 55, in Quang Nam Province on August 7, 1969. In the background, soloist PFC Marcus Barnes is singing "How Great Thou Art."*

Ruth and I leave Marble Collegiate Church with President and Mrs. Richard Nixon.

With our eight grandchildren.

TOP: *For many years I have regularly conducted my NBC radio program "The Art of Living."*

BOTTOM: *On May 27, 1988, Ruth and I opened the Center for Positive Thinking. Joining us in the ribbon-cutting ceremony were John Y. Brown, Phyllis George Brown, our daughter Elizabeth, and Art Linkletter, who had served as building committee chairman.*

Carl was completely puzzled at these references to a wedding anniversary, for Dressen was not one to show sentiment, and he figured the manager was killing time to let another pitcher get to the mound. Instead, Dressen said, handing him the ball, "You're my man, Carl. Finish this game before dark."

So the game was resumed with the Dodgers behind one run, and nineteen Yankee batters to come to bat, the greatest hitters in baseball, but not one got a hit! The game went to eleven innings, and Carl and his teammates won, 6–5.

In another game in midsummer the temperature was pushing a hundred degrees. Carl Erskine was tiring and felt under pressure, but he had a technique for handling pressure. He believed we have a reservoir of memories of peaceful scenes and places to draw upon in a crisis. In that moment he went back in memory to Indiana and Lake Webster where he was fishing early one morning. The water was like glass. Suddenly he heard sounds of singing and chimes. It was a hymn, "All Hail the Power of Jesus' Name," coming from a church camp. The memory steadied him, peace overcame his tiredness and his sense of pressure, and he pitched with restored power.

When Carl came up to the Dodgers in 1948, he and Betty came regularly to my church in New York. In a sermon I used an illustration about Branch Rickey, who was general manager of the Dodgers. The couple spoke to me after the service. Giving me his name, Carl said, "You talked about my boss in your sermon."

"Are you the Dodger pitcher?" I asked. We have been friends ever since.

At another time at church he was dressed in a blue suit, sitting with Betty in the balcony. An usher tapped him on the shoulder and asked him to assist in taking up the offering. "You were in the bleachers, Carl," I said, "and you performed as well as on the mound."

Carl always had affection and admiration for his teammates. He particularly admired the way in which Branch Rickey and Jackie Robinson broke the color line in baseball. "Jackie was militant about injustice, but he showed great self-control in those tumultuous days. Rickey knew that Jackie's mother was a dedicated Christian," said Carl, "and Mr. Rickey had great respect for a mother's influence." He believed Jackie would respond to insults like a Christian, and he did, turning the other cheek and proving his power. In so doing he became a baseball immortal and a great American.

CHAPTER 7

The Sixties: A Turbulent Decade

AS the sixties began, Amos Parrish, perhaps the greatest merchandising expert of the era, was the speaker at a dinner in our Marble Collegiate Church in New York City. He was a brilliant thinker and speaker, and his topic that night was "The Sizzling Sixties." Mr. Parrish, a positive thinker and optimist, figured that everything would go forward with power in the new decade. Well, things sizzled all right, but it was in an unexpected manner, for it turned out to be the decade of youth rebellion. But the American people have the capacity to handle trouble creatively. And the United States came out stronger than ever.

The census of 1960 showed that the population of the United States was nearly 180 million—179,323,175, to be exact. One interesting and significant fact was that the number of women in the work force had risen from 25 percent in 1940 to 34 percent in 1960.

The struggle against racial bias was stepped up by "sit-ins." It started in Greensboro, North Carolina, when four black students from a local college refused to move from a lunch counter when denied service. This led to "wade-ins" at southern beaches, "read-ins" at libraries, and "kneel-ins" at racially segregated churches. At various cities in the South, where the "sit-in" and other forms of "ins" occurred, race riots broke out. Black leadership stressed the policy of nonviolent protest.

In 1962 James Meredith became the first black student ever to register at the University of Mississippi. But the campus was said to have been littered with broken glass and signs of an angry crowd protesting integration. It was all indicative of a troubled decade. In the integration struggle a notable illustration of the bad feeling engendered was when Governor George Wallace of Alabama stated he would stand in the schoolhouse door to block integration. But despite the governor's opposition, federal officials made it possible for black students to register at the University of Alabama. Progress was being made in racial justice. In the sixties this principle was established through conflict and trouble, for old opinions and customs sometimes die hard.

Another problem was that any new device always seemed to be feared and questioned. In this case it was the introduction of computers. The question was asked, "Will computers rob people of their jobs?" In spite of this, the great computer age began.

Edward R. Murrow, my friend and neighbor on Quaker Hill at Pawling, New York, one of the great radio and TV reporters of the era, exposed the filth, despair, and poverty of millions of migratory farm workers. The brilliant reporting and compassion of Ed Murrow was intended to affect the conscience of Americans, and it did.

On November 8, 1960, Senator John F. Kennedy was elected president in a very close contest with Vice President Richard M. Nixon. Not until noon the next day could the outcome of the election be determined. In fact, Kennedy won the presidency by a plurality of less than one-half percent, or less than two votes per precinct. But once he was elected, the American people rallied unitedly behind him. His attractive appearance and charm of manner made Jack Kennedy a natural in the television age.

The inauguration took place on January 20, 1961, in twenty-two-degree weather before an enthusiastic crowd. They cheered President Kennedy's inspired line, "Fellow Americans, ask not what your country can do for you. Ask what you can do for your country."

I knew John Fitzgerald Kennedy only slightly. He came quickly to the presidency and, tragically, his administration was short. He was a brilliant man, and the younger generation felt he was truly their representative. He had a charming personality and great energy, and he was a stout defender of liberty. He said the United States will "pay any price, bear any burden, meet any hardship, support any friend, oppose any foe to assure the survival and the success of liberty."

President Kennedy, on May 11, 1961, sent additional military advisers to South Vietnam to help a local army of over three hundred thousand oppose the Communists.

The Soviet Union had gone ahead of the United States in space exploration with the orbiting of the earth by Yuri Gagarin in April 1961. But in May 1961, Alan B. Shepard, Jr., became America's first man in space. He was cramped into a Mercury capsule and was weightless for about five minutes, but long enough to peer down at the Caribbean and exclaim, "What a beautiful view" before parachuting down into the Atlantic. President Kennedy had the long view. He said, "I believe this nation should commit itself to achieving the goal of landing a man on the moon before this decade is out."

A year later, John Glenn became the first American to make an orbital flight. He whirled around the globe three times and made a safe landing in the Atlantic Ocean. I remember following Glenn's flight and recall the greeting from Perth, Australia, when he flew over that city and commented, "Oh, that view is tremendous." At times grave doubts were expressed about the heat shield working when he entered earth's atmosphere. It did work, and we remember his courage in facing such an uncertainty.

In April 1962 President Kennedy made the steel companies back down from an announced price increase. In excoriating terms the president accused them of "public irresponsibility in their pursuit of private power and profit." He stated that steel's action in increasing prices was "virtually traitorous" at a time when he was asking unions to withhold demands for wage increases.

Other happenings and trends are interesting. An indication of how the decade might go was the frenzied reception of a new dance step called the "Twist." Newspapers commenting on it said, "If proof is needed that we're out of the 1950s, it is 'the Twist' that is sweeping the nation."

A student movement or revolt in the sixties was a phenomenon never before experienced in the United States. It was perhaps basically a protest against the Vietnam War but was never a rebellion as such, where mobs storm the government with intent to unseat it. It is true that youth, mostly college students, burned draft cards, the national flag, and some buildings. And they marched and shouted and generally disrupted public assemblies, such as church services and university commencements. But it was not really revolution, for they made no moves to attack the legally constituted authority of the United States government.

Very few refused to register for the draft for military service. The revolt was mounted against prevailing American culture, against an entity called "the establishment," toward American business, the capitalistic or free enterprise system. It was, to some extent, a protest against the moral standards handed down from puritan forefathers and the longtime customs of polite society.

One of the mildest and oddest manifestations of the quasi revolution was hair. There was even a Broadway musical called *Hair.* This movement was against hairstyles of the older generation, against gentility, against the establishment. And the revolt against hairstyle was accompanied by a wide spread "dressing down," not only of youth, but of "liberal" adults as well. No longer did attractive young women appear on the streets, well groomed and dressed beautifully. They tried to look down-dressed by wearing soiled white sneakers, oversized men's jackets, stringy hair, and blue jeans deliberately made to look dirty, old, and ragged.

Young men grew bushy beards, wore their hair long, scuffed around in sandals, and seemed dedicated to establishing marijuana as the drug of choice.

During the decade of the 1960s I was much on the road on speaking engagements. One morning I boarded a plane to Chicago and took my seat. Soon a "hippie," down dressed, with long hair, came in and flopped down in the seat beside me. "Good morning," I said.

To my surprise he greeted this civility by saying, "What's good about it?"

I made no comment, and he opened the morning paper, glancing at headlines, turning the pages impatiently. Meanwhile, I was editing a book manuscript. Suddenly I was interrupted by a violent snort from my young seatmate. He crumpled his newspaper with a profanity, "G—— d—— lousy world," and sat back in disgust.

It happened to be a beautiful, sunny morning. A few gentle cumulus clouds floated in a serene blue sky. Pointing toward the outside with the thumb of my left hand, I said, "Looks pretty OK out there."

He glared and grunted a contemptuous, "Huh."

I went on with my work, and he just sat. Then suddenly he said, "Mister, mind if I ask you a question?"

"Ask away," I replied.

"Why do you wear your hair so short?"

"Because I'm a rebel," I said. "Nobody, and I mean nobody, is going to tell me how to wear my hair."

He replied, "I suppose you don't like the way I wear my hair?"

"Was I so impolite as to comment on your hair?" I asked. "You are a free American and can wear your hair any way you want to." Then we both lapsed into silence.

Again my young friend posed a question, somewhat politely this time. "I suppose you are of the establishment."

"Your supposition is in error," I answered. But he was not to be stilled, and I was glad, because my pastoral instincts were to reach him with my faith, and I felt that so far I hadn't done very well. But soon he gave me an opportunity.

"Mister, tell me one more thing. You actually seem happy. I don't run into many happy people. Are you putting on an act? Are you really happy?"

So I said, "This time I want to ask you a question. Do you really want to know why I'm happy, or do you just want to give me an argument?"

"No, I really want to know because for some reason you interest me."

"Well," I said, "in that case I'll tell you. But hold onto your seat, for this may rock you. And I'm going to insist that we don't argue about it. Take it or leave it. OK?"

"OK," said the young man.

"I can answer your question about why I am happy in one word of five letters, and this is going to throw you, so hang on. And remember, don't give me an argument. My answer is— Jesus."

By this time, we were rolling up to the gate at O'Hare Airport. The young man turned and, surprisingly, shook my hand and mumbled something under his breath that sounded like, "I may try that sometime." Then he was gone.

As for me, I thought I might have handled the conversation better than I did, but then I knew that Jesus, even in the 1960s, understood how to handle people.

On June 17, 1963, the Supreme Court banned prayer in public schools on the grounds that it violated the First Amendment to the Constitution. This decision raised a storm of criticism and protest all over the country.

The assassination of a president always shocks and wounds an entire nation. Such was the grief when the popular young president, John F. Kennedy, was violently struck down.

On November 22, 1963, I was in my office at the *Guideposts* magazine building in Carmel, New York, when the incredible news came that the president had been shot while driving in an open car in Dallas, Texas. We were informed that he was in the hospital and surgeons were feverishly trying to save his life. At once I spoke to our employees over the public address system, asking them to stop work and to pray for President Kennedy. Following silent prayer, I offered an appeal to God for him. But I learned afterward that the president was shot at 12:35 P.M. and at 1:00 P.M. was pronounced dead.

All have read the story of how the assassin's shot rang out from a building, killing the president and seriously wounding Governor John B. Connally, riding in the same car. Fortunately, Governor Connally recovered.

The momentum of our mighty governmental system continued, and one hour and twenty-eight minutes later, Vice President Lyndon Baines Johnson, who had been riding several cars back in the motorcade, took the oath of office on Air Force One as the thirty-sixth president of the United States. Standing beside him as he took the oath was the late president's widow, her dress spattered with the blood of her martyred husband.

I first met President Lyndon B. Johnson when I spoke to a national convention in Chicago. They were honoring the distinguished world traveler and broadcaster, Lowell Thomas, my friend and neighbor in Pawling, New York. The president was seated in a large chair on the platform, and as a speaker I was seated beside him. As tributes were being given to Lowell, President Johnson whispered an aside to me: "Lowell Thomas taught me much about elocution." I was impressed by the remark, for *elocution* is a word seldom used nowadays to mean public speaking. It was a kind of a return to my college days, for when I took a course in public speaking, it was called "elocution." I liked Lyndon Johnson. He was a brilliant man and very likeable, with his down-to-earth and homey style. He said as he was leaving, "Dr. Peale, you might say a prayer for me. I could sure use it." He impressed me that day as harassed and tired.

Five years later, on June 6, 1968, the late president's brother, Senator Robert Kennedy, died by an assassin's gun in Los Angeles. It was just two months after the great civil rights leader Dr. Martin Luther King, Jr., was shot and killed by an assassin in a Memphis, Tennessee, motel. Dr. King had received the Nobel Peace Prize just three years earlier.

The book *Chronicles of America* carries an account of the march to Montgomery, a dramatic incident in the integration struggle, saying,

> *More than 25,000 people poured into Alabama's capital to-day, affirming the right of Negroes to vote. With the protection of federal troops, Negroes accompanied by sympathetic whites marched 54 miles from Selma to the capitol building. The Rev. Dr. Martin Luther King, Jr., addressed the crowd from the capitol steps with the flag of the Confederacy waving overhead. . . . On March 6, state troopers, some on horses,*

waded into a group of marchers. The sight on the television
news of marchers being beaten and trampled has stunned the
nation. (p. 807)

I personally knew both of these outstanding leaders. Martin Luther King, Jr., revered black leader and powerful speaker, made one of the greatest speeches in American history to an audience estimated at two hundred thousand in Washington, D.C., on August 28, 1963. The symphonic reiteration of "I have a dream" will, I believe, long live in the annals of our country.

Assassinations, race riots, the hippie movement, the war in Vietnam, and student protests of that war kept the sixties embroiled, though some progress was made in racial justice. But in recording all these troubling events, which is quite necessary in any treatment of the sixties, perhaps it is well to relieve the reader (and the writer, also) by some lighter-hearted material.

Writing a book is much like writing music. The great composers in writing symphonies used the method of first putting a slow (largo) serious movement before a quick (scherzo) light-hearted movement, thereby giving relief from tension and stress in the musical score. This, of course, gave the same relief to the listener. Additionally, there was always the big climax at the end, where the same chord is struck again and again (Beethoven always did this) so you know it is the end!

So I want to tell about the family dinners we had at home at 1030 Fifth Avenue when our children Margaret, John, and Elizabeth were growing up. Once one of them said, "Tell us a story, Daddy."

The others chimed in and Ruth said, "If you can't remember one, make one up." And so I did.

One story, with a new chapter told each evening, was called, "Larry, Harry, and Perry and their magic airplane." Harry always carried a miniature airplane in his pocket and when any of the three suggested going somewhere, Harry would take the plane out of his pocket, mumble the mystic words, "Heebie-blinken and jeebie," and their miniature plane would immediately grow large. Then Harry, Larry, and Perry would take off on an adventure. I must have "made up" a couple of hundred versions of where they went on their excursions.

I told another story with the uninspired title of "Jake the Snake." Later our grandchildren demanded the same stories and, since they were never written, I had to make them up all over again.

Probably I could never even have imagined one of the greatest true stories of the sixties. It was about a boy named Neil Armstrong and another boy named Edwin Aldrin, Jr., landing on the moon, of all places. Of course, Harry, Larry, and Perry never dreamed of going there. Neil Armstrong was from Wapakoneta, "Wapauk," as all of us native Ohioans used to call it. On July 20, 1969, Neil Armstrong landed on the moon. The astronaut said of his feat, "That's one small step for man; one giant leap for mankind."

A story went around that as a little boy, Neil sat on his front steps in "Wapauk" looking up at the full moon and telling all who would listen that he was going up there sometime. Along with Neil Armstrong I spoke once at a dinner meeting in Columbus. At the time I didn't think to ask him if that story is true. I hope it is.

During the turbulent sixties there was an appalling and apparently uncontrollable rise in crime. We experienced the menace of drug abuse. We witnessed the beginning of a wave of pornography—historically a grim sign of decadence—that seemed to affect the whole country and continues to grow, in drama, movies, and literature. And we saw the rise of antireligious activism, with self-appointed zealots working, sometimes successfully, to ban school prayers or bar any reference to Deity in public ceremonies.

All in all, it was a troubled decade, with confusion and disenchantment dominating the national scene. I was often dismayed by the tension and anger and divisiveness that seemed to prevail.

But if the state of the nation during the 1960s left something to be desired, our private lives continued to be exciting and fulfilling. The first half of the decade saw all three of our children happily married, and in the second half grandchildren were arriving, if not in droves, at least in satisfactory numbers.

Margaret married Paul F. Everett, a dynamic young minister, and went to live in Pittsburgh. They have two children, Jennifer Ruth and Christopher Peale Everett.

John Peale, working for his doctorate in philosophy and teaching at the same time, married Lydia Woods, who presented him with three new additions to the Peale clan: Laura Stafford, Charles Clifford (named after his great-grandfather), and Sarah Lacy. In the fall of 1965, Elizabeth, who after graduating from Mount Holyoke College had worked as a researcher for the *Reader's Digest*, married John M. Allen, a senior editor of that magazine. Since Ruth and I had bought another home on Quaker Hill at Pawling, New York, John and Elizabeth purchased our previous home, Sugar Tree Farm, on Quaker Hill and soon had two little girls and a little boy of their own growing up there: Rebecca Belknap, Katheryn Ruth, and Andrew Peale Allen.

One other pleasant event during these years was the appearance of a motion picture, *One Man's Way*, based on my biography, written in 1958 by my great friend Arthur Gordon. Don Murray, who played the part of the young minister, came to Marble Collegiate Church to hear me preach and to study my delivery and mannerisms firsthand. Eventually television rights were sold, and the movie has appeared in many reruns across the nation.

My work load was tremendous, but I liked it that way. Between 1960 and 1970 I published six more books. My newspaper column and radio broadcasts continued to reach millions, and my speaking schedule to national business conventions and community public meetings was as crowded as ever.

Two of the most significant aspects of my life were *Guideposts* magazine and the Foundation for Christian Living. In 1970, celebrating its twenty-fifty anniversary, *Guideposts* moved into an ultramodern, 2-million-dollar publishing center in Carmel, New York. Leonard Peale, the younger of my brothers, had joined the *Guideposts* staff as director of special projects. Circulation was approaching the 2 million mark, and we had five overseas editions (Chinese, Korean, Thai, Latin American, and British). In a time when some well-established magazines were in financial trouble and a few disappeared altogether, the dynamic interfaith magazine *Guideposts* continued to grow and prosper, proving the theory that the best road to success is to "find a need and fill it."

The magazine's contents faithfully reflected major changes in the religious climate of the country, especially the "Jesus revolution" of the late 1960s. But the chief emphasis remained, as always, on the dramatic, true story of faith at work in ordinary people's lives. Books, records, films, Christmas booklets, and television programs broadened still further the magazine's remarkable outreach. As it moved into its second quarter-century, the demand for its message seemed as strong as when it first appeared just after the Second World War.

The growth of the Foundation for Christian Living was just as spectacular as the expansion of *Guideposts*, and in a way even more remarkable, since it depended entirely on voluntary contributions. From the start Ruth masterminded it all.

The Foundation's vital statistics reached astounding proportions. Each month the printed messages were reaching a "congregation" of a million people in 110 different countries. The Foundation was sending out yearly some 25 million pieces of mail. It was receiving letters at the rate of more than two thousand per day. Some of the letters sought advice, others asked for prayers, some simply enclosed contributions as a wordless token of gratitude. A building program doubled the amount of office space available but still was barely enough.

Expenses mounted steadily—but so did contributions. There's nothing else like it in the history of publishing—or religion!

In addition to all other commitments, I became president of my denomination, the Reformed Church in America, in 1969-70. Also I served as president of the Protestant Council of the City of New York, an organization of some eighteen hundred churches. I held this post for four years—longer than any predecessor.

In my busy speaking schedule I have shared the speakers' platform with many gifted men and women and often appeared with them on programs. Paul Harvey, who is famous for "the rest of the story," is one of the speaking geniuses with whom I have had the pleasure of a friendship.

Another is Art Linkletter, one of the most beloved men in America. Upon being introduced, Art would come out on stage with that big smile of his and talk to the people. He fascinated them with his spirit and his humor, and he impressed them with his wise advice about how to live.

I have known many pastors and preachers, and I think the ministry in the United States is a profession of which all Americans should be proud—for the clergy's fidelity, honesty, love, and good example of character.

I have often preached for Dr. Robert Schuller in his great

Crystal Cathedral in Garden Grove, California. Having known him since his earliest years, I am impressed by the fact that he has now become, in effect, a pastor to the world, since his TV program is beamed to many foreign countries. He is a genius in organization and one of the greatest preachers of our time.

I remember so well the time I preached for Dr. Schuller when he was holding services in a drive-in theater before his present church was built. I drove down from Los Angeles to Garden Grove on a Sunday morning to keep my engagement. My picture was tacked onto telephone poles. He had a big crowd assembled for the service, many listening through audio boxes in their cars and others of the congregation gathered around the platform.

Bob advanced to the edge of the platform and said, "I assume that all who have assembled here think that the greatest person present here today is Dr. Peale. I want to announce that he is not by any means the greatest person. The greatest person here today is Jesus Christ, your Lord and Savior."

That remark affected me so deeply that I said to myself, "Robert Schuller is 100 percent all right." And I loved him from that minute on, for he had in mind the basic essential ingredient of Christianity.

Bob came to see me one day when plans for the Crystal Cathedral were just beginning to be formed. In his character-istically enthusiastic way, he described it to me so clearly and lucidly that I, too, became enthusiastic. I said, "Bob, that great church is already built in your mind. Now all you have to do is to collect the money to build it out of steel, stone, and glass," which he did very soon after that.

The year 1968 brought a happy occasion. In the autumn of that year, during the presidential campaign, Richard Nixon versus Hubert Humphrey, I received a visit from two young people,

Julie Nixon and David Eisenhower. "Dr. Peale," said Julie, "we want you to do something for us."

"Of course," I said cheerfully. "What?"

"Marry us," they both said at once.

"Marry you?" I declared. "Certainly. I will marry you two at any time, anywhere! Who knows about it?"

"No one," they said, "except our parents. And now you."

"Where will the wedding be? In the White House?"

"No," Julie said, "right here in this historic church. I've loved it ever since I was a little girl. And David loves it too."

Julie made it clear that she considered marriage a sacred relationship and a wedding a religious ceremony, which should be held in church. Determined not to have her own wedding turned into a public spectacle, she asked me to keep their plans secret until the time came for a formal announcement.

I promised that I would, and I did, but neither Ruth nor I foresaw the pressure that would be exerted by the media. The engagement of these young people, members of two of America's best-known families, was finally announced, but not the date of the wedding or the place. Speculation at once reached a feverish intensity. Where would the wedding be? Who would conduct the ceremony?

For the next six weeks I could scarcely answer my own phone; Ruth and my secretaries had to screen all calls for me. Inquisitive reporters besieged my office day and night. False rumors were everywhere. One morning, when Ruth and I were in Phoenix, Arizona, we turned on a popular TV breakfast show and heard to our amazement and amusement that *Women's Wear Daily* had broken the story: the Nixon-Eisenhower wedding was to take place in the Cathedral of St. John the Divine.

This "scoop" was soon proved false, but even after the correct plans were announced, the pressure persisted. Reporters swarmed around like bees, demanding endless details, none of which Ruth was at liberty to divulge. To placate them she finally held a press conference, conducted a tour of Marble Collegiate Church, and gave facts about its long and distinguished history. This hardly satisfied the reporters. "Mrs. Peale," one of them said resignedly, "you can talk more and give less information than anyone I ever listened to!" Others tried to involve her in a discussion of what sort of marriage counseling I might be giving to the young couple. When that failed, a persistent female reporter said, "What would you do, Mrs. Peale, if a certain young couple brought a marital problem to you?"

"I'd refer them to my husband," replied Ruth serenely.

One Sunday when the president-elect and his family, along with Julie's fiancé, attended the early service at Marble Collegiate Church, Julie, who had brought her own Bible, asked if she might talk to me between the services about various details of the ceremony. She wanted to use the Quaker "thee" in certain passages, and she had also picked out her favorite Psalms, the 100th and the 121st. She and David were closeted so long with me that her father—waiting with his wife, Pat, and Ruth in the outer office—began to fear she might delay the second service. He was about to knock on the inner office door, but his wife dissuaded him. "Relax, Dick," she said. "Remember, you may be president-elect of the United States, but here you're only the father of the bride."

"I know," said the next president of the United States with a sigh. "I tell you, I can cope with the inauguration all right, but to get through this wedding is something else!"

Elaborate security precautions had to be taken before the rehearsal, which lasted over two hours, and before the wedding itself. Secret Service men were everywhere. Closed circuit television coverage was arranged so that David's grandfather, former President Eisenhower, could watch from the hospital bed in Washington where he was confined. Since the ceremony was held on Sunday, December 22, 1968, at 4:00 P.M., the church was beautifully decorated with Christmas wreaths and greenery and banks of poinsettias. The wreath behind the altar was almost fourteen feet in diameter. Julie and her mother attended the morning worship service. Everything went off perfectly, and for the Peales the day was doubly exciting because our daughter Elizabeth and her husband brought their first child to the church to be baptized, Rebecca Belknap Allen.

On January 20, 1969, Richard Milhous Nixon was inaugurated president of the United States, a month after Julie's wedding. A few months later, Ruth and I were invited to the White House. While we were there, a suggestion was made that led me into one of the most exciting and memorable experiences of my life—a presidential assignment in Vietnam.

It was a rainy Sunday in June 1969. President Nixon had been in office only a few months. One of the innovations he had made at the White House was to have simple, nondenominational religious services on Sunday mornings, to which about three hundred guests were invited. On this day—Father's Day, 1969—I had been asked to preach.

At the White House an aide conducted Ruth and me to the First Family's living quarters on the second floor, where President and Mrs. Nixon greeted us and chatted for a few minutes over coffee. Then the president led the way down to the East Room of the White House, where the service was to be held. At the appropriate time, he introduced me and I gave a fifteen-minute sermon, "Be Glad You Have Problems."

After the service there was a reception where the president and Mrs. Nixon shook hands with everyone. Ruth and I, also in the receiving line, were impressed with the diversity of the guests: Supreme Court justices and cabinet ministers, members of the White House staff, secretaries and telephone operators, some with their children. The president seemed to know them all by name and had a pleasant word for each. One old gentle-man told him in a quavering voice that the last time he had been at a White House reception, as a small boy, he had shaken hands with Teddy Roosevelt.

"What impressed you most?" President Nixon wanted to know.

"His beautiful striped trousers," replied the guest promptly.

The president looked down at his own sober dark suit and laughed. "Times have changed," he said with a smile.

After the reception, Ruth and I were invited to a family lunch in the private dining room on the second floor of the White House. Both of the president's daughters, Tricia and Julie, were there, also Julie's husband, David Eisenhower, his mother, Mrs. John Eisenhower, and her daughter Barbara. A fire was laid, and the president, who loves open fires, asked an attendant to light it.

Conversation was animated, the young people joining eagerly in discussions that ranged across the whole spectrum of national and foreign affairs. And it was in connection with one of these topics that the president suddenly told me, "Norman, I have a job for you."

Although I did not have the faintest notion of what President Nixon might be going to say, I replied that I would be happy to do anything I could.

"What I'd like you to do, Norman," the president said, "is go to Vietnam. Talk to our troops there, boys in the field, boys on some of our naval vessels, boys in the hospitals. Give them the same type of inspirational message that you give us Sunday after Sunday in church. Cheer them up; make them feel that the people back home haven't forgotten them but really care about them and appreciate what they're doing. Do you think you could find time for an assignment like that?"

For a moment, a wave of conflicting emotions swept over

me. I was touched and flattered that the president should think so highly of me and of my ability to reach and help people. I had missed the excitement and privilege of serving my country as a military chaplain in World War II. I knew that any assignment in a war zone carried an element of danger. How would I stand up to the experience of flying over jungles full of hostile guerrilla fighters or visiting outposts under fire? For perhaps a second I hesitated. Then I pushed all doubt out of my mind and told the president calmly that Ruth and I were already planning a round-the-world trip and would be glad to stop over in Vietnam and do whatever such an assignment required.

"Good," said the President. "I'll set it up with our military people. You'll hear from the secretary of defense. And I think you'll find it a memorable experience."

It was, indeed. First, Ruth and I flew to Japan, where I followed an exciting pattern of international speaking engagements. Next we went to Taiwan, where President Chiang Kai-shek and Madame Chiang had invited us to stay at their summer palace high up in the mountains. There, at a formal dinner in our honor, I happened to ask Madame Chiang how her husband managed to stay so youthful looking and alert despite his great age.

"He does it by prayer and meditation," Madame Chiang replied. "He devotes thirty minutes to prayer three times a day."

Next morning I happened to wake up very early. I went to the window and looked out into the chilly mist. What I saw made me call Ruth. Across a courtyard on a balcony a tall robed figure was pacing slowly up and down, followed by a great dog. It was Chiang Kai-shek at his morning devotions, drawing strength and inspiration from his deep Christian faith.

From Taiwan we flew on to Hong Kong, greatest bargain city in the world for shoppers. Then on to Bangkok, where Ruth was to wait while I carried out the Vietnam assignment.

The next four and a half days were the most crowded and in many ways the most meaningful of my life.

At home in the United States a wave of antiwar protests was sweeping the country. At the University of Chicago hundreds of students charged the offices of administration and lodged there for several days. In City College of New York a mass of students chanted down the president of the college and camped outside his office door. Mobs of radical students rampaged over Columbia University for a week. But I thought, as I lived with the troops in Vietnam, that little thought was given them by war protesters. I dislike the fact of war and believe it will ultimately be outgrown, but that happy situation in the present state of world affairs is not yet existent.

Army chaplain Col. Hans E. Sandrock was assigned to me as chief aide and guide. A small military jet airplane picked me up in Bangkok and flew us to Saigon, where I received the first of several military briefings. Then I was whisked to a guest house known as "The White House," where visiting VIPs were given comfortable accommodations. Throughout much of my stay in Vietnam, I wore olive drab army fatigues with "Rev. Peale" lettered above one jacket pocket and the single word "Pastor" above the other.

In the summer of 1969, American military presence in Vietnam was at its height, under the command of General Creighton Abrams. After reading endless accounts in the American press of destruction and devastation in South Vietnam, I was prepared to find Saigon practically in ruins. I was amazed to find almost no signs of war at all. It was a busy, crowded city that reminded me of New Orleans with its wrought-iron balconies and handsome residences behind tall iron fences.

Hundreds of bicyclists pedaled through the streets. Shops offered every type of merchandise. I was struck by the beauty of the women, with their dark eyes and lustrous hair, many wearing a long white garment over black slacks that reached to their ankles and created a very graceful effect. I asked my guide if such women had any contact with the American troops. "Probably not," said Sandy Sandrock. "These are very conservative, highly respectable people who live their own lives within their own culture."

As a representative of the president, I was given a three-star security rating. This meant that every time I flew in an army helicopter, three other 'copters went along as protection. I first noticed this on a visit to an American pacification team at an outlying village, where we found a lively game of baseball in progress between a mixed group of Americans and Vietnamese. A black sergeant from North Carolina interpreted a speech of welcome made by the Vietnamese headman of the village. Then he showed me what he and his men were doing for the villagers in terms of sanitation, health, and education. "Most of our people over here," the sergeant said, "aren't fighting—they're building. When I finally get out of the army, I plan to come back here and make helping these people my life's work."

At a dinner given for me by General Abrams, the same emphasis was stressed. "You'd never know it from reading the *New York Times*," one high-ranking officer said, "but our presence here is really building a new civilization. All the media back home seem to report is the negative side of this war. I wish they'd talk once in a while about the hospitals and schools that our troops have sponsored!"

I was impressed by General Abrams, a man of firm opinions, but also with a gentler side that revealed itself in his love of classical music and fondness for serious books. At the dinner he spoke out strongly against the pornography that seemed to be engulfing the United States, and especially against the degradation of the American stage—sentiments that I heartily endorsed.

I was equally impressed with Ambassador Ellsworth Bunker, who also entertained me at his residence, a fine old house that had once belonged to a prominent French family. Again the high ceilings and revolving fans reminded me of New Orleans. The table was set in the garden, with flares flickering against the tropical shrubbery. White-coated Vietnamese servants moved quietly to and fro. The guests—all male—included several Vietnamese senators. Knowing of the constant danger of assassination attempts, I asked my host how he could be sure the Viet Cong might not try to infiltrate the embassy staff. "I take all reasonable precautions," said the courtly, white-haired ambassador. "Beyond that, I live without fear."

In that peaceful setting the war seemed far away. It seemed much closer when I visited the wounded in various hospitals. Many beds were empty—a sight to gladden the heart—but many were occupied. On entering a ward, I would ask military companions to remain behind because I wanted to visit these boys as a simple civilian pastor and talk to them without any protocol or constraint. I would stand by a bed and ask the occupant, "What's your name, son? What happened to you? How are you feeling?"

Always the answers were cheerful, optimistic, upbeat. They felt fine; they felt great; they wanted to get back to their outfit; they wanted to finish the job. I saw hundreds of men and spoke with dozens. Not one complained. Not one criticized the army. Not one was antiestablishment.

"I can hardly believe all this," I said to one hospital chaplain. "How do you account for all the negative reports that are printed in the States or carried on TV back home?"

The chaplain shrugged. "I once asked a reporter why he wrote such slanted copy," he said. "The man told me that if he didn't he would lose his job."

One such reporter asked me what my "investigations" had revealed so far.

"I'm not here as an investigator," I told him quietly. "I'm here as a pastor to help anyone who needs my help, that's all." The reporter looked disappointed and moved away.

A highlight of my Vietnamese trip was a visit to the great aircraft carrier *Kitty Hawk*, on combat station off the coast. I flew first to the huge American airbase at Danang, then transferred to a small navy jet capable of landing on the flattop's deck. The plane was piloted by the admiral's own pilot, the admiral himself being on board the *Kitty Hawk*. I could hardly have been in better hands. As they strapped me into a complicated harness and fitted me with a Mae West life jacket, I asked perhaps a bit apprehensively just what all these precautions meant.

"Oh," said the pilot, "there's nothing to landing on a carrier. There are five arresting cables stretched across the flight deck. Even if we miss the last one, we can always go around again." I then observed his protecting helicopters. The pilot said, "They are just in case we go into the drink."

"Does anyone ever fall in the drink?" I wanted to know.

"Hardly ever," said the pilot. "And chances are, a helicopter will be able to fish you out if you do."

Not entirely reassured, I watched a tiny speck on the horizon grow into a mighty floating airdrome, carrying upwards of five thousand fighting men. Large as it was, the landing area looked alarmingly small against the vastness of the sea. Skillfully the pilot made his approach. Wheels touched the deck. There was a terrific jolt as one of the cables caught the hook. To my considerable relief, we were down—intact.

Waiting in white uniforms were the captain and some of his officers. Since at sea the captain remained constantly on the bridge, he had made his quarters available to me, complete with mess boy ready to bring me anything I wanted. Dinner that night was in the admiral's quarters. After dinner I was to address the crew.

They assembled, hundreds of them, in the fo'c'sle, a huge area between decks. Sailors perched on cranes, on windlasses, on stanchions. Under the sun-heated metal, even at night it was fearfully hot. While I waited to be introduced, I watched the admiral's crisp uniform turn into a sodden, shapeless mass of cloth. I could feel the sweat trickling down my own back. When I did stand up to speak, and tried a gesture or two, I found myself swishing perspiration in all directions.

But I forgot my discomfort when I began to speak. I told listeners that I had asked the president what message he wanted to send to the men fighting this unpopular war so far from home. "The president said to me, 'You tell them that their country loves them, and their president loves them—yes, tell them that God loves them.'" At the end, the applause was tremendous, and dozens of the men crowded around, wanting to shake my hand.

Later that night I went up on the bridge and watched as combat planes took off, and others, their missions completed, came winging back like homing pigeons. At one point the captain was informed that a plane was overdue, and I felt the tension that gripped the whole ship until the welcome word came that the missing plane had been spotted by radar. I had little sleep because all night long it sounded as if huge chains were being dragged about the metal deck just over my head. Up early for good-byes, I found that taking off from a carrier is even more hair-raising than landing on one.

"They catapult you off," I told Ruth later. "That's fine, but nobody told me that the plane then begins to sink before it picks up speed. It seemed to me that we sank forever before we began to climb again!" It was during this takeoff that I noticed the lips of one of my chaplain friends moving silently.

"Were you praying?" I asked him later.

"Sure," replied the chaplain promptly. "Weren't you?"

I was indeed.

Most unforgettable of all my experiences in Vietnam was the service I conducted for the Seventh Marine Regiment on Hill 55, far up in the combat zone. The marines had seen hard fighting and had suffered heavy casualties. The service was to be a memorial to the men who had died.

First I flew to the headquarters of the Third Marine Amphibious Force, where I was welcomed by Major General Ormond R. Simpson, commander of the First Marine Division. Then the general and I flew on to Camp Muir on Hill 55, the home of the Seventh Marines. There in a shack I was introduced to several marine chaplains, each of whom described his job. One said casually that one of his duties was ministering to an outpost twenty miles away—just a squad of men, but to get there he had to walk the whole distance through mine fields and under fire, never knowing if the next step might be his last.

"Did you volunteer for this duty?" I asked.

"Yes," said the chaplain. "I volunteered."

"Why?"

"Because I became a priest to serve the Lord Jesus Christ and His children wherever they might be."

"What denomination are you?"

"Catholic."

"Are you happy in this work?"

The chaplain smiled. "I wouldn't be anywhere else for anything in the world!"

Later I said to Ruth, "I really felt unworthy in the presence of such men. They're tremendous—just tremendous."

We left the shack finally and went up Hill 55. At the top a

simple altar had been set up between the flags of the United States and South Vietnam. It was hot, but a breeze fluttered the flags. Seated on the ground were perhaps seven hundred marines in full combat gear, all with their rifles. All around were sandbagged fortifications. In front of the altar was an M-16 rifle, inverted, with its bayonet thrust into a single sandbag. On top of the rifle was a helmet, symbolic of those who had died in combat.

From the hilltop the ridges and rivers of the region were plainly visible. "That's the infiltration route over there," General Simpson said, pointing across the valley where bombers were at work, the sound of the exploding bombs clearly audible. He went on to indicate different areas that the troops had named: Dodge City, Arizona Territory, Oklahoma Hills, Pipestone Canyon.

The service began. A military band played. The soldiers sang the old majestic hymns: "Nearer, My God, to Thee" and "My Faith Looks Up to Thee." A chaplain read from the Scriptures and offered a prayer. Sitting beside the general, I was so deeply moved that I wondered if I would be equal to this assignment. In a moment of doubt and hesitation I turned to the general. "What do you want me to say to them?" I whispered.

The general was staring at the ground. "Why ask me?" he replied. "Some of the men of this regiment have died. Others will die. All are in great danger. This may be the last time some will ever hear the name of Jesus Christ or receive a Christian message. Tell them about patriotism. Tell them that their country is worth dying for. Tell them that freedom is worth any price. Say anything you want. But tell them about our Savior."

As I always do before speaking, I prayed silently for help and guidance. Then I stood up and faced the tired, patient faces of the Seventh Marines, many of them just boys. I spoke first about the somber hills and valleys and canyons around them and the names they had given them. Some day, I told them, some of those names might be enshrined in American history alongside such names as Lexington and Bunker Hill, Bull Run and Gettysburg, Chateau-Thierry and Belleau Wood, Guadalcanal and Iwo Jima . . . all the places where American men have loved their country so much that they were willing to give their lives for it.

Next I spoke to them of their fallen comrades. "You knew those men," I said. "They didn't want to die. They hoped, each one of them, to go home some day, to walk the tree-lined streets of some quiet American town, to see their parents and their sweethearts or their wives again. Now they have sacrificed all that, but their sacrifice is testimony to a dream. The dream is that we're going to build on earth some day a state of affairs where men will live together in love and peace and harmony regardless of racial origin or national background or any difference. In other words, the way Jesus Christ intends his kingdom to be."

As I spoke, the lines of a poem came into my mind. On my way to the service on Hill 55 I had thought the poem might be suitable, but I had been unable to remember all the words. Now, suddenly and effortlessly the words came to me. It was written by Winifred M. Letts, an Englishwoman, half a century ago and half a world away, but appropriate still:

> *I saw the spires of Oxford*
> *As I was passing by,*
> *The grey spires of Oxford*
> *Against a pearl-grey sky.*
> *My heart was with the Oxford men,*
> *Who went abroad to die.*
>
> *The years go fast in Oxford,*
> *The golden years and gay,*
> *The hoary Colleges look down*
> *On careless boys at play.*
> *But when the bugles sounded—War!*
> *They put their games away.*

They left the peaceful river,
The cricket field, the quad,
The shaven lawns of Oxford,
To seek a bloody sod.
They gave their merry youth away
For country and for God.

God rest you, happy gentlemen,
Who laid your good lives down,
Who took the khaki and the gun
Instead of cap and gown.
God bring you to a fairer place
Than even Oxford town.

A deep hush had fallen on the men seated on Hill 55. There was no sound except for the snapping of the flags and the dull explosion of bombs far across the valley. In that silence I felt closer to my audience and closer to ultimate reality than ever before in my life.

"In the solemnity of this moment," I said, "we must face the fact that you are the ones who are called upon to endure the stress of battle. You are the ones who must bear the heat and burden of the day. May the good God, your heavenly Father, and your Savior Jesus Christ watch over you and protect you and keep you from harm. But if, in the uncertainties of battle, the moment comes when you too are called to go forward with your fallen comrades, may you meet it bravely and know that your soul is clean at the last, and that another life is just beginning for you. And may we who are older and cannot fight the battles everlastingly keep faith with you, so that together we shall turn not only our own beloved country but the whole world into a place of peace and good will.

"As for those who have died here, we can say about them the greatest thing that can be said about any mortal man: Greater love hath no man than this, that he lay down his life for his friend."

I walked back to my seat through a profound silence. Nobody stirred. When I looked at the general, I saw tears on that tough marine warrior's face. A black soldier with a magnificent voice stood up and sang "How Great Thou Art." A squad of riflemen fired a volley. A bugler played "Taps." The service was over.

There was no time to linger; the hilltop was too exposed. The officers did not like to keep the men so concentrated; they had to get back to their posts. Within a week, although I could not know it, many of those men, including a battalion commander, would be dead.

I shook hands with all the officers. Then I climbed into the helicopter, whose rotors were revolving, and strapped myself into my seat. But then on impulse I unfastened the belt, stood up, and went to an open hatch in the rear where I had an unobstructed view. Just below me the general and the seven hundred men and officers of the Seventh Marines were drawn up at attention, saluting me. I felt my throat tighten. Not knowing exactly how I should respond, I raised my hand and waved. Instantly the rigid lines dissolved and fourteen hundred hands waved good-bye in return.

I watched until they were out of sight. Then I went back to my seat, put my face in my hands, and wept like a child.

I close this chapter with a final personal note. I shall never forget the ending of the decade of the 1960s, for my brother Bob died just short of the year 1970 and just before his seventieth birthday.

Bob—Robert Clifford Peale, M.D.—was two and a half years younger than I, and we were inseparable from childhood on. Boys who picked a fight with either Bob or me soon learned that they had to take on the other brother too. Bob became a doctor of medicine, a graduate of Harvard Medical School. He was on the staff of Christ Hospital in Cincinnati and later practiced in Olean, New York, and Pawling, New York.

When practicing medicine in Pawling, he lived near the Foundation for Christian Living, where we saw each other almost daily. He would wave good-bye with a characteristic gesture. And for all our years together after I became a minister, he always called me "Deacon."

After he died I was inconsolable, until one day when I was speaking to a meeting of employees of the Foundation, and suddenly I "saw" him clearly and distinctly, striding across a plaza between our building and his house. It was all perfectly real. He looked to be about forty years of age, in the prime of life, healthy and energetic. He waved with the old-time gesture and the same smile that I knew so well and seemed to say, "It's all all right, Deacon. It's all all right." I was so moved that Bob had returned for several seconds to tell his brother that the afterlife was indeed "all right." In life he was a believer and he had found his beliefs confirmed. And he was still watching over me as he had always done in mortal life.

CHAPTER 8

The Seventies: "Better Days Are Coming"

THE decade of the seventies began with Ruth and me going up, and I mean really going up, to the top of one of the greatest mountains in the world, the Matterhorn. With us was our longtime friend Arthur Gordon. And a pilot, too, for we were in a helicopter. It was August 12, 1970, and the flight lasted only an hour—from eleven o'clock to noon, but the memory of it lasts a lifetime. Ruth told the story in her book *The Adventure of Being a Wife*, and I will quote from her account:

> *We were in one of our visits to Zermatt, a little town in Switzerland that nestles in a valley at the foot of the Matterhorn. This gigantic spire of jagged granite looks like a great knife thrust into the sky. The summit is more than 14,000 feet above sea level. Not far away is the Monte Rosa, highest mountain in Switzerland, but its approaches are more gradual and it's not so dramatic. The Matterhorn stands alone, brooding, somber, pockmarked even in summer with ice and snow. For years the natives believed that it was the home of devils or evil spirits who could hurl thunderbolts or fling down great boulders upon any humans who dared to come close. Someone once said that the Matterhorn isn't just a mountain; it's a "presence." It is. . . .*

During our visit to Zermatt . . . we stayed in the chalet of an old friend, Theodore Seiler, a Swiss banker and president of Seiler Hotels. Ted Seiler grew up in Zermatt. His grandfather owned the first hotel there, the Monte Rosa, where [the Seiler family] still welcomes guests. It was to this hotel that Whymper [the first man to climb the Matterhorn] returned from his triumphant but tragic climb [on which three men died]. A bronze plaque near the entrance commemorates the event.

Ted Seiler told us that, next to climbing the Matterhorn, the most dramatic way to view it was to fly around it and over it in a helicopter. He added that a pair of helicopters, flown by German pilots, was kept on the alert at all times on the outskirts of Zermatt. There was a small one that could carry four persons, and a larger one that could take six. They had already made several highly dramatic mountain rescues. Ted Seiler said that if the weather was right, he might be able to arrange for us to make a mountain flight over the nearby peaks and glaciers. He said that if we did, we'd never forget it. [How right he was!]

It sounded exciting, all right, but also a little scary. I had been in a helicopter only once in my life, to view some farm acreage. But Norman, on the trip he made to Viet Nam at the request of President Nixon, had made many helicopter flights. . . .

All through the first part of our visit, the weather was uncertain. Much of the time swirling clouds shrouded the Matterhorn. When they would part momentarily, we could see that the slopes around the great peak were covered with fresh snow. But the pinnacle itself was too steep for much snow to cling to the jagged rocks.

The night before our last day in Zermatt, the wind switched to the north—a sign of fair weather, Ted Seiler said. Sure enough, the next day dawned sparkling and bright. The sky was a deep, cobalt blue—not a cloud in it. Golden sunlight poured down on the streets of Zermatt, gay with banners and colored awnings and window boxes full of petunias and geraniums. . . .

A telephone call was made to the heliport. . . . We were told that if we would come there at eleven o'clock, there was a good chance that we could make the flight. The big helicopter was undergoing repairs, but the small one was operational. Since there would be room for three passengers in addition to the pilot, a writer friend of ours [Arthur Gordon] who was also in Zermatt said he would like to go. . . .

Shortly [we] found ourselves standing on a huge square of concrete about half the size of a football field. A painted circle with a large H in the center was evidently the target for descending pilots. Through the open doors of a hangar we could see the large red machine being worked on. We were told that the smaller helicopter was off on patrol but would return shortly. . . .

We sat in the brilliant sunshine, waiting. . . . My feelings were a mixture of excitement, anticipation, and a little apprehension at the thought of soaring off the friendly earth in a plastic bubble supported by nothing but a pair of ungainly windmill blades and a single engine.

As we waited, we talked about Whymper and mountain climbing and the strange and dangerous things people seem to do in their quest for happiness. . . .

Our ears picked up the pulsing drone of the helicopter before our eyes saw it. Then suddenly there it was, hovering like a gigantic dragonfly. The pilot swung around into the wind. With a roar and buffeting gusts of the cool mountain air, the machine settled onto the concrete platform. The pilot cut the engine. The whirling blades gradually ceased revolving and grew still.

The fuel tanks were refilled. Certain mountain-rescue equipment was taken out to make room for us. Almost before we knew what was happening, Norman and I were fastening our seat belts in the rear seat. Our friend sat forward, on the left. The young pilot, relaxed and self-assured, was on the right. . . .

"Where do you want to go?" [he asked.]

At this the station manager standing on the pad spoke to the pilot through his open window. It was in German and I could not understand, but a resistance on the part of the pilot and then a shrug of the shoulder by the pilot as the station manager insisted, gave me a tremor of apprehension. Was he being asked to push this helicopter beyond its limit in order to show us the glorious mountain?

The doors swung shut. The pilot adjusted his earphones and spoke a few words in German to the controller inside the hangar. His right hand held the stick. With his left, he twisted the throttle between the two forward seats. The helicopter vibrated, stirred, began to lift. Suddenly, with a heart-stopping lurch, it seemed to me that we simply jumped off the concrete platform into thin air. There was no forward taxiing, as in a conventional aircraft. We leaned into the wind—and leaped!

Up the little valley we rushed, not more than two hundred feet off the ground. The pilot and the passenger in the front seat could see almost straight down; I was glad we couldn't. On the instrument panel I could see the air-speed indicator; the needle was hovering between forty and fifty knots. The altimeter indicated that we were about six thousand feet above sea level, and climbing.

Up the valley we flew, between towering rock walls on either side, past lacy waterfalls, over green meadows filled with mountain wild flowers. The helicopter banked steeply and started back, still climbing.

Below us, now, we could see Zermatt spread out like a toy village, its chalets and hotels dominated by the spire of the church. We were following the contours of the ground to the east of the town. Once or twice it seemed to me that our rate of climb was too slow to enable us to clear the ridge just ahead, but we always slid over with something to spare. Far below I could see the orange cars of a funicular crawling along, like ladybugs, between pylons. Now the dark hues of the evergreens were giving way to the browns and grays of the rugged terrain above the timberline. Ahead and to the left was a cluster of buildings marking the terminus of the cog railway that climbs steeply up from Zermatt to Gornergrat, some ten thousand feet above sea level, a favorite lookout point for tourists who want to view the whole majestic panorama of glaciers and Alpine peaks.

But few tourists ever saw them as we were seeing them now. Moments later we were over the Gorner-glacier itself, a huge river of ice, blinding white, strangely scored and indented. Where it ended, a torrent of water, gray with glacial sediment, poured from under the wall of ice. To our right, a lordly peak, the Stockhorn, pierced the sky. The altimeter now read eleven thousand feet, and some dim unwelcome memory reminded me that as a rule pilots are not supposed to fly above ten thousand without oxygen. We had no oxygen.

Up the glacier we raced at sixty knots. Tortured and barren as the ridged ice was, I was glad to have it there, only a couple of hundred feet below. If our engine stopped, I told myself cheerfully, we could just sit down on this nice solid ice and wait to be rescued—perhaps by a friendly St. Bernard. But then, looking ahead, I saw that the glacier ended. And not just the glacier, but the mountain, the world, creation ended. Rushing toward us was a fine white line, sharp as a knife blade. Then nothing. Just a kind of livid emptiness.

Over the line we went straight out into this awful chasm. I felt my feet pressing against the floor, as if by doing so they could somehow hold us back. Beneath us the precipice fell sheer, straight down, for more than a mile. We hung suspended over a stupendous void, ringed by the great peaks, floored by purple shadow. . . .

My rational mind knew that we could fly just as well over a mile of nothingness as over a glacier, but my stomach didn't seem to know it. My stomach, in fact, seemed to have stayed back over the glacier. I saw that [Arthur] had reached for the side of our plastic bubble as if to brace himself, and I knew he too was wondering what four infinitesimally small and unimportant human beings were doing in such a sublimely terrifying place.

Only the pilot seemed unconcerned. We swung behind the twin peaks of the Monte Rosa, still higher than our heads although our altimeter now indicated twelve thousand feet. Below us a few ants seemed to be toiling painfully across the vast snowfields. Climbers. "That can be dangerous," said the pilot, pointing at them, "unless you know what you're doing. There are snow bridges that can break. See those holes that look like caves? If you fall in one of those, you're finished. No one can get you out!"

He spotted something lying on the crest of one of the ridges, something that might have been a man lying in the snow. "Better take a look." The helicopter banked steeply; the rotor blades made a flat, thudding sound as they bit into the air. I clutched Norman's hand. "Just a tent," said the pilot as we swept over the object. "Sometimes climbers will try the Monte Rosa one day and the Matterhorn the next and spend the night down there." I tried to imagine what it would be like underneath that tiny piece of canvas with the wind moaning in the icy blackness outside. My imagination wasn't up to it. . . .

The Matterhorn is impressive at a distance. Close up, it is overpowering. And we were close, so close that it seemed to me we could see the cracks in the towering walls. But when the pilot pointed out some climbers, they looked unbelievably tiny, just dots of color clinging to the naked rock. Past a small hut we went, perched like an eagle's nest on the edge of a stupendous precipice. "Climbers spend the night there," the pilot said. "They start climbing at dawn."

We were still climbing ourselves, in a tight spiral that circled the Matterhorn three times. It seemed to me that our engine was laboring in the thin air. I was beginning to feel some shortness of breath, and I could see that Norman was too. Now the altimeter read fourteen thousand feet; we were almost on a level with the summit. I could see clearly the iron cross that marked the spot where Whymper and his companions had stood so long ago. Higher still, so that we could look down on the summit itself. There on that dizzying height, three tiny figures stood, waving at us, and I felt a sudden surge of admiration for the restless, unquenchable spirit of adventure that had made them challenge and conquer those frowning heights. Perhaps our generation was not so soft and effete after all.

Then we were dropping down through the luminous air, the great mountain receding behind us. "Swallow hard," the pilot said. "It will ease the pressure on your ears." Zermatt came into view, tranquil in the sunlight. The landing pad looked like a linen handkerchief. We made one last turn, came up into the wind, settled down exactly in the center of the painted circle. The flight was over.

But the experience wasn't over. I stepped from the helicopter walking on air. I was exhilarated as never before. The world had a glorious radiance and wonder about it. I looked at Norman and Arthur. Their faces were alight. This tremendous upsurge of spirit stayed with us for days.

> *Our friend Ted Seiler had arranged for the [horse-drawn] hotel van to meet us. The two splendid horses trotted back to the village, bells jingling gaily. We sat in the old coach . . . not saying much. The spell of the heights was still on us, and the transition from twentieth-century helicopter to nineteenth-century horse-drawn van was so abrupt and so strange that it seemed unreal.*
>
> *All through the rest of that day, and many times since, I have found myself reliving the exaltation of that moment when we swept over the edge of the glacier into the vast emptiness, and the thought has come to me that perhaps dying is like that; an outward rush into the unknown where there is nothing recognizable, nothing to cling to, and yet you are sustained and supported over the great void just as you were over the comfortable and familiar terrain.*
>
> *Fanciful? Perhaps. But I remember that when we said our prayers that night, thanking God for the privilege of seeing all we had seen, and also for our safe return, it didn't seem fanciful. Not at all.*[1]

Early in 1970 the every-ten-year census was taken. The population of the United States had reached 203,184,772. The major increase was in the South. New York State, for the first time, had to take second place to California, which had 20 million to New York's 18.2 million people.

The radicalism of the 1960s lingered on as the general attitude of the 1970s. Long hair persisted, and even earrings became a men's style. In a national poll on marriage in the 1960s, 24 percent had considered marriage obsolete. In 1971 34 percent of Americans were saying marriage was obsolete.

But at the same time the play *Jesus Christ, Superstar* was a box office success.

Another evidence that the turbulent sixties were still carrying over into the 1970s was that some student antiwar protestors burned a bank near the University of California at Santa

---

[1] Ruth Stafford Peale, *The Adventure of Being a Wife* (New York: Prentice-Hall, 1971), 77-86.

Barbara. A rock-and-bottle-throwing rampage ensued amidst cries of "Burn, baby, burn!" and "Death to corporations!" Some in the crowd had cooler heads and objected to the violence, saying these actions had "no relevance to issues."

This brings to mind an incident that happened at the White House on January 23, 1972. Ruth and I were there for a dinner celebrating the fiftieth anniversary of the *Reader's Digest*. The guests of honor were the founders and publishers of the *Digest*, Mr. and Mrs. DeWitt Wallace. After dinner all the guests went to the East Room for the presentation to both DeWitt and Lila Wallace of the Medal of Freedom and to enjoy a concert by the famous musician Ray Conniff and his singers. He had prepared a concert including favorite songs of the past fifty years in honor of the Wallaces.

Ray Conniff had sixteen of his most accomplished singers scheduled for this important engagement, but one took ill and a substitute had to be engaged at the last moment. At the front were seated President and Mrs. Nixon and DeWitt and Lila Wallace. Ruth and I were just behind the Nixons and the Wallaces, and we could clearly see what happened.

The chorus came on stage. Then a young woman in the front row of the singers suddenly pulled out of her bosom a large banner that had been hidden under her long dress. On it in large letters it said, "Stop the bombing in Vietnam!" She added vocally, "You go to church every Sunday, Mr. President. Act like a Christian." The guests were aghast at the impropriety and brazen impoliteness of the girl's actions. Also, everyone realized that if she had had a gun under her dress, she could have killed the president at that short range.

As Ray followed the singers on stage, guests began shouting, "Throw her out!" And security guards quickly escorted her out of the room.

Ray Conniff, my friend for years, handled the situation

masterfully, as did the president. The concert went on. Later Ray said, "Mr. President, I am terribly embarrassed. The singer was a substitute recommended by someone in whom I had confidence."

The president, who hadn't batted an eyelash during the incident, said, "Ray, forget it. Things like this happen to me often." Then the president, ever a positive thinker, said, "Besides, if this hadn't happened, the only ones to know Ray Conniff had a White House concert would be the few present tonight. Now the whole world will know."

Afterward Ray told me that this young woman had first turned down this engagement to substitute, but when she told her friends who, like herself, were hostile to the government and the president, they urged her to accept it as a "great chance to get a message to President Nixon."

Ray Conniff is not only famous for his musical leadership but is also a believer and a positive thinker. Recently he reminded me of the time he and his wife, Vera, were trying to arrange financing to buy and reconstruct an old, rundown farmhouse in Switzerland. He was thinking about these difficulties on an airplane from Los Angeles to New York, when he saw me on the plane and asked my advice. I told him not to think negatively of the difficulties but to think positively about them and to thank God for His blessings.

Later Ray told me that he walked into his bank with a financing proposal that Swiss friends said would never be accepted and made his offer. The bank manager looked at him silently for long minutes and finally said, "All right, I think we can arrange matters your way." Ray said he saw then that the idea of positive thinking really worked. Many of the good things in life happen to us when we think right.

That first year of the seventies a major tragedy occurred on May 4 at Kent State University, Kent, Ohio. Governor Rhodes ordered the National Guard into Kent after dissident students threw bottles at police, and firebombs were thrown into the offices of the ROTC (Reserve Officers Training Corps). Newspapers of the day said the nervous guardsmen moved on a student antiwar rally that was being held despite its having been banned by the state administration. When the students refused to obey the order to disperse, the national guard fired tear gas at the crowd.

The students then hurled rocks at the soldiers. At this moment soldiers of the guard heard a shot, so it was said, and nervously let go a volley, killing four and wounding ten. Students later said that the dead were not attending the rally but were bystanders. This event shocked the nation. It was said to be the result of a heated mixture of ideas: opposition to the war, inspired by Communists, a mistaken notion that violence is a valid way to convey an opposed opinion, and finally a nervously activated attack and killing of excited young Americans.

A commission appointed after the Kent State tragedy found that students who bomb and burn are using improper methods to express political opinions and urged the president that "he must solve a political crisis that has no parallel in the history of our nation." The commission also said, "Derisive rhetoric must end or the survival of the nation will be threatened."

In these hectic, hate-filled times of the seventies the government, represented by the army, marines, and national guardsmen, arrested, on May 3, 1971, approximately seven thousand demonstrators in Washington, D.C., herding them into jails and even commandeering the coliseum and a football field. These actions were taken on the belief that the capital was in danger.

In all my years I have assumed that the government at Washington will stand whatever else happens. Was it ever actually threatened, even in these troubled times? I do not think that it was, for the American people love their country too much to allow their elected government to be overthrown. And the student revolution of the sixties and seventies, with all the rock throwing, flag burning, draft-card burning, and other signs of protest, never did envision the destruction of our free government.

And the government did stand, notwithstanding all that went on, including the many events that finally led to the incredible resignation of the president of the United States on August 9, 1974, and the succession of Vice President Gerald R. Ford to the presidency. As he succeeded to the vice presidency, my friend Nelson Rockefeller said the final word to all the agitation and turmoil: "There is nothing wrong with America that Americans cannot right."

On May 7, 1975, President Ford declared, "The fall of Saigon closes a chapter in the American experience. I ask all Americans to close ranks, to avoid recrimination about the past." This was to say that the Vietnam War was over. It was entered into to stop the victorious march of Communism but was only partially successful. It is interesting to realize that what war could not do, peace did about twenty years later when the Berlin Wall came tumbling down like Humpty Dumpty. One country after another that had been Communist-governed for forty years threw off the yoke and declared for freedom, democracy, and free enterprise. Communism was worn out, an ignominious failure.

My first meeting with Jimmy Carter occurred when he was governor of Georgia. *Guideposts* magazine gives an award each year to a church that is doing an exceptional form of service. "The Church of the Exceptionals" in Macon, Georgia, was the one designated that year. It was a church for handicapped people, but in Macon they called them the exceptionals, for they do exceptional things.

Ruth and I went on stage to meet the chairman of the

NORMAN VINCENT PEALE

meeting and Governor and Mrs. Carter. Five big, old-fashioned rocking chairs were on the platform. I was seated next to Governor Carter; Ruth was beside Mrs. Carter.

The auditorium in Macon, seating 10,000 people, was full, and the stage was fitted up to represent an altar with lighted candles. One gigantic candle in the central position was unlighted. To the accompaniment of soft organ music a young man, perhaps seventeen years of age, was brought down the main aisle in his wheelchair. He was in an advanced spastic condition and had been designated to light the large candle. When he reached the front, someone handed him a lighted taper with which to light the large candle. This proved very difficult because of the spastic reaction of his arms when extended. The entire audience seemed to strain with him in his futile efforts to apply the taper to the candle.

I noticed that Governor Carter was especially tense, leaning forward in his chair, hands on his knees. I heard him offering a prayer in no more than a whisper, but because of my nearness, I could hear his words, "Oh, dear Lord, please help that poor boy to light that candle." When the taper finally met the candle and it was aflame, the governor fervently said, "Thank God." This gave me an insight into the character of this good Christian man—his caring, compassionate nature. Later, when he was our president, I found myself praying for him in his vast responsibilities. I always admired him as a man.

In 1976 America joyfully celebrated the two hundredth anniversary of its birth as a nation in 1776. Tall ships, over two hundred of them, sailed into New York Harbor. President Ford rang the old Liberty Bell in Philadelphia. In many cities and towns actors staged replicas of the battles of the Revolutionary War. Fireworks everywhere lighted the summer sky.

Every state and indeed all cities, towns, and villages had ceremonies to honor our country's bicentennial. It was a year

202

of pride in citizenship in our great free land, of review of our glorious history, and of anticipation of our equally glorious future, which every positive-thinking American fully expected.

I received a letter from Governor Rhodes of Ohio, saying he was inviting several distinguished Ohioans to return to their native state for a special celebration dinner. And to my surprise and, I must admit, pleasure, he was including me among them.

I had previously been honored by receiving the "Christopher Columbus Award" from the city of Columbus, Ohio. This I greatly appreciated as a native Ohio boy. But I was not prepared for the high-sounding award presented to me by Governor James Rhodes at this bicentennial dinner in the state's capital city. The governor, in a felicitous speech, presented to several of us, including Neil Armstrong, first man to walk on the moon, and Lowell Thomas, famous broadcaster, and others, "The All-Time Great Ohioan Award." You can be sure this unexpected and generous award is prominently displayed in our Center for Positive Thinking in Pawling, New York.

The New York Council of Churches designated a Sunday when a layman would give the sermon, rather than the minister. Always cooperative, I asked Henry J. Kaiser, the well-known industrialist, to take over this assignment. The next year I invited the famous author Dale Carnegie to speak. After two years this practice was given up. I never did find out why. I thought it a good idea.

In opening his sermon, Henry Kaiser said, "This morning I found Mama [meaning his wife] weeping. Concerned, I asked her why she was crying. Between sobs she replied, 'Oh, it's because I'm so happy, for this morning Papa is going to be in the pulpit preaching a sermon.'" Later he told me that when he was a young man in a poor family in Utica, his mother wanted him to become a preacher. Apparently his wife had similar feelings. He was an exceptional personality, and he gave an inspiring talk.

Dale Carnegie, writer of famous motivational books, has taught more people to speak in public than anyone else. Like Kaiser, he drew overflow crowds. Dale was talking about faith and about his mother, when suddenly he stopped. I was near enough to see he was emotionally overcome. He had been telling how poor they were, so poor that sometimes the family did not know where the next meal was coming from. At such times his mother would always say, "The Lord will provide." And, said Dale, "He always did." Then he added, "He always will." It was at this moment that he could not speak for a long moment of emotional remembrance. These two "sermons" by two of the most famous men of the century were unforgettable.

As one who was spanked in the Greenville, Ohio, public schools for printing "'16" (our class numerals) on the high school sidewalk, I was interested to note in my research for this book that the Supreme Court on April 19, 1977, ruled "that spanking children does not violate Eighth Amendment protection against 'cruel and unusual punishment.'" My punishment may not have been cruel. Certainly it wasn't unusual. It was just plain painful. I couldn't sit down for a week.

The famous illustrator Norman Rockwell died at the age of eighty-four at his home in Stockbridge, Massachusetts, on November 8, 1978. He was universally admired and loved. He did 322 covers for the *Saturday Evening Post* between 1916 and 1963. He portrayed Americans with understanding and patriotism, and pretty much as we are.

As much as we love our country, most people would perhaps agree that something needs to be done about certain problems. Marriage, for example. I think it was an old Roman who said, "The empire begins at the fireside." Certainly the strength of a nation is derived from the home. Family statistics in 1979 showed the divorce rate up 69 percent in 10 years, with the average marriage lasting 6.6 years; and 40 percent of the children born in the seventies spent some of their youth in a one-parent home. I was fortunate to be born in the closing years of the nineteenth century when the home was secure and marriage was for life.

In 1977 Elvis Presley's death marked the end of his rule as the "king of rock 'n' roll," a position he had held since the 1950s. Presley had a voice touched with southern blues. When the parents of the nation first heard him sing, they decided they didn't want their teenagers to hear him. And when they viewed his physical gyrations on the Ed Sullivan Show, they would gladly have kept their children from seeing him, as well. Nevertheless, his music captivated a whole generation. In 1990, *Time* magazine rated Elvis Presley one of the leaders of the twentieth century. He died at age forty-two, apparently of a drug overdose, although the official death report listed "cardiac arrythmia."

Good things were going on in the world as the decade neared its end. President Carter engineered what was hailed as a diplomatic miracle when he brought President Sadat of Egypt and Prime Minister Begin of Israel together. And to add further to the good news, President Carter, with the aid of Cyrus Vance, then secretary of state, signed SALT Treaty II with Soviet Premier Leonid I. Brezhnev.

I recall one day years ago in Bellefontaine, Ohio, in a high school class hearing our history teacher make a statement that struck me at the time as, shall I say, fanciful but at the same time prophetic. Professor Guy Detrick was more than a starry-eyed idealist. He had served several terms in the Ohio legislature and was a thinker touched by perception. He said, "You young people listen to me. Before some of you die the world will be a different place, with international differences being settled by peaceful negotiations, not by recourse to war. I won't live to see it, but some of you will." I think this good Christian teacher was given the privilege of a glance beyond the horizon of history to see a great world. Maybe, just maybe, it is dawning now.

Living in New York City, as Ruth and I have since 1932, we have met many people, not only from the city but from all over. For example, the late Governor Herbert Lehman of New York became a good friend.

Members of my church wanted to have a special service to celebrate my having been on Fifth Avenue for ten years. The committee to plan the event was in my study and somebody said, "I think we should get the governor to make a speech."

"Oh, you couldn't get the governor," another man said.

And yet another agreed. "The governor doesn't know us."

So I spoke up and said, "I know him and like him very much."

"Even so, Norman, I bet you five dollars you can't get him to come down from Albany to New York on a Sunday night."

"Keep your money, Jack, you're too reckless with it," I said.

Jack asked, "How are you even going to reach him?"

"See that telephone?" I replied. "I think the governor also has a phone. Let's call him up."

One man looked at his watch and came up with a further negative: "He wouldn't be in his office at seven o'clock in the evening."

"We can try." So after getting the telephone number of the state capitol in Albany, I placed a call.

A man answered, and I asked, "Is the governor still around? I'd like to talk with him."

The man at the other end mumbled something I couldn't quite get. Then he came back on. "Yeah, he's in his office. I'll put you on with his secretary."

After thanking him, I heard a man's voice say, "This is Herbert Lehman. Who is this and what can I do for you?"

I told him, and he became very personal.

"Glad to hear from you, Norman. Haven't seen you since that meeting where we all got heckled."

"Wasn't that something?" I agreed. "That fellow wasn't very sober."

"He was drunk," the governor said, adding, "I've probably seen more drunks than you have."

Before I go on with this story, you might like to know about the meeting the governor referred to. He and a couple of well-known political figures were speakers at a big meeting. I can't recall why I was there, but I was the fourth speaker.

A man in the audience, an obviously rough kind of fellow, stood and heckled every speaker. When it came my turn, up rose this fellow and he asked, "Rev., what are you doing with a bunch of politicians?"

"That is a good question, my friend," I replied. "If I tell you why I am with them, will you be a good fellow and let me go on with my little talk?"

"Yeah, OK, that's a deal."

"Well," I said, "as politicians they are a bunch of sinners, and I'm trying to work on them." The audience laughed, the politicians laughed, the heckler laughed, and he was quiet the rest of the evening. After I sat down, the governor said, "You loved the fellow, and so you won him."

Well, to get back to the governor on the telephone, he asked, "What can I do for you?"

I told him, and he said, "Sure, I'll come."

He did, and the congregation loved him just as I did.

At the end of the decade, television had come a long way since its early development. On March 1, 1979, the *Washington Post* took a poll to ascertain the opinions Americans had regarding TV. The resulting news article said that "99 percent said they had a TV set, but only 17 percent said the programs were better than five years ago and 41 percent said they were worse. The *Post* found TV watching had declined, with 54 percent watching less than five years ago. More than a third said they would pay a small fee to get rid of commercials, which they found too long, loud, and untrue."

As the decade progressed, there were plenty of problems. But the only people I ever knew who had no problems were in the cemetery. The country that has run out of problems has run out of steam. Problems are a sign of life, and the United States was very much alive as the decade came to an end.

On November 4, 1979, a mob of Iranian students seized the U.S. Embassy in Teheran, taking ninety hostages. Ayatollah Khomeini, who had taken over leadership after the shah had been deposed, seemed to support the students' action. The shah was hospitalized in the United States at the time. A few hostages, mainly women, gained their freedom as the year ended, but fifty-two remained in captivity.

Toward the end of his administration, President Jimmy Carter made a television speech in which he said, "The nation has spiralled downward into self-doubt and low self-esteem." He called for Americans to "recapture their old spirit of self-reliance." He was so right in appealing to Americans to recover the attitude that had made us the greatest nation in the world—a positive attitude, belief in ourselves, self-reliance; in other words, to drop the "we can't" attitude and go back to the positive American "we can" spirit.

I close this chapter with an illustration of how we tend to become what we think. I remember talking to a teacher who was driving me to a "positive thinking rally." He talked enthusiastically about students who had been rescued from failure and dropout-ism. One story I remember was about a boy named Mike, whose school attendance and grades were worsening. He was developing a surly disposition together with a tendency toward low self-esteem. He was exhorted, lectured, and punished, but to no avail. Finally he landed in the superintendent's office with the teacher's recommendation that he be expelled from school as unreachable and therefore unteachable.

The superintendent tried talking with Mike but elicited only negative response. Finally the superintendent sat quietly studying the boy, who stolidly awaited the verdict. To the lad's surprise the school superintendent said, "Mike, hold out your hands." Mike, surprised, held out his hands. The educator took them in his hands. "Mike," he said excitedly, "you've got wonderful hands, long and slender but strong, which is surprising for your stocky build. Boy, you've got the hands of a surgeon. Maybe that's what you are intended to be. Get going, Mike, and good luck." He said nothing about punishment, let alone expulsion. It was genuine motivation, esteem, admiration.

What about Mike? He went slowly and thoughtfully out of the building and sat on the steps, examining his hands, turning them over and over and seeing things he had not even sensed previously. He came back to school the next day and was there every day. Gradually everyone sensed a new spirit in this previously "couldn't-care-less" guy. His grades picked up. He graduated from high school, then college, and later (you guessed it) from medical school.

"Did he become a surgeon?" I asked, fascinated by the story of Mike.

"One of the best," the superintendent answered.

CHAPTER 9

The Eighties: Decade of Energy and Action

THE eighties very literally began with a bang, for on May 18, 1980, Mount St. Helens in the state of Washington erupted with a gigantic explosion and rumble that registered 4.1 on the Richter Scale. The volcano hurled about a mile of earth and ash into the air. Destruction was widespread. Scientists said it would be a decade before the surrounding country recovered from this mighty demonstration of the vast power of Mother Nature.

There had been another disaster on April 24, 1980, though that time it had not been by an act of nature. President Carter, who like all Americans wanted the hostages in Iran freed, ordered a rescue attempt by the military. But on that day a helicopter collided with a transport aircraft in a remote desert location, killing eight Americans. The mission was terminated, but at least an attempt was made to free the American hostages.

In 1980 Ruth and I took our entire family, seventeen in all, to Europe. We went to Geneva, Interlaken, Zermatt, Austria, Munich, and the picturesque village of Oberammergau to witness the world-famous Passion Play. The events leading to Christ's crucifixion are acted out on a stage open to the weather, with actual mountains as a backdrop. People come from all over the world to see this reverent story of the Lord's suffering and crucifixion.

On the streets many languages are spoken. Villagers are selected for the various parts. Thousands crowd into the auditorium and watch the Passion Play all day, except for a noontime break. The effect upon the viewers is like no other I have ever experienced, and Ruth and I have attended the Passion Play at Oberammergau five times. You find yourself actually living with the Savior as the scenes of His passion are enacted before you. I have seen big men sobbing as the action unfolds. Poignantly the words come, "Father, forgive them, for they know not what they do." And a silent and reverent multitude departs at the end, everyone uplifted by the narrative of that one solitary life.

During this time *Guideposts* magazine was having a spectacular growth, climbing to number twelve among America's most widely circulated magazines.

There is a rule of thumb in the publishing business that to determine readership one multiplies by four the paid circulation. On this basis *Guideposts*, with approximately 4 million paid subscribers, has the astounding total of approximately 16 million readers every month. Our research indicates that, indeed, every copy of *Guideposts* is read by four persons, making it the most widely read religious and inspirational periodical in the world and perhaps in history, too. And *Guideposts* continues the policy of taking no advertising.

My wife, Ruth, is president of the magazine, I serve as chairman, and together we are copublishers and editors-in-chief. Van Varner is editor.

Ronald Reagan was elected president of the United States over President Carter on November 4, 1980, in a victory of landslide proportions, winning 489 electoral votes to 49 for

President Carter. George Bush was elected vice president.

Within minutes after Ronald Reagan had been inaugurated president of the United States on January 20, 1981, the fifty-two hostages were on planes from Iran, bound for West Germany, after 444 days of captivity and mistreatment. President Reagan asked former President Jimmy Carter to go to Wiesbaden to meet the hostages on his behalf. Following a long meeting with the former prisoners, Mr. Carter reported that many of them had suffered worse treatment than had been believed—such as being subjected to mock firing squads.

Two days after the hostages returned to the United States, they and their families were invited by President Reagan to a reception at the White House, and they were honored in every section of their country.

On March 30, 1981, President Reagan was shot by twenty-five-year-old John W. Hinckley, Jr., as the president was leaving the Washington Hilton Hotel after speaking to a labor convention. Upon arrival at the hospital the president told Nancy, his wife, "I forgot to duck." Most severely wounded in the shooting was the presidential press secretary, Jim Brady. It was reported that the president's pastor called to see the president in the hospital and in the conversation asked, "Mr. President, did you know you might have died in that attack?"

Mr. Reagan answered, "Yes, I know that."

"Were you afraid to die?"

The president is said to have replied, "No, for I have a Savior."

Unfortunately, another assassination attempt against a prominent world figure was more successful. Anwar Sadat, president of Egypt, was assassinated on October 6, 1981, while reviewing a military parade in Cairo. Several men dressed in uniform burst from the ranks and started shooting at the reviewing stand, wounding many and killing several, including

President Sadat. The attack was apparently not part of an intended coup. It was assumed to be in resentment of Sadat's signing of a treaty of peace with Israel.

As the reader may remember, I was once a newspaper reporter and ever since have admired unusual stories. Besides, as a preacher and speaker with the responsibility of producing sermons and talks that are designed to effect change and stimulate action, I have searched newsprint for interesting stories that I could use to help make strong people out of weak persons. I found among my papers a clipping from the old, now defunct, *New York World Telegram* entitled "Builders Top Nature, Turn Sand into Stone":

> *What would take nature a million years, the builders of the new 60-story Chase Manhattan Bank building are doing in a few weeks.*
>
> *With the aid of common chemicals pumped down into the earth, they are turning an underground pocket of quicksand at the construction site into stone.*
>
> *"It's almost as simple as it sounds," declared Andrew Fisher, the Chase Manhattan's building consultant. "The Chemical Soil Solidification Co. sinks pipes down to the quicksand and forces a solution of sodium silicate and calcium chloride through them. In just a few days the quicksand is changed into sandstone.*
>
> *"The sandstone isn't very hard," said Mr. Fisher, "but it's solid and watertight, and it solves one of our biggest foundation construction problems."*
>
> *The quicksand lies at the east end of the bank site near Liberty St., sandwiched between a layer of hardpan earth and bedrock.*
>
> *"We have to dig down to the bedrock to put in the foundations for the new bank," said Mr. Fisher, "and the quicksand presented quite a problem. We had to seal it off to keep it from pouring into our excavation and—more important—to prevent the undermining of nearby buildings."*
>
> *The conventional way of handling the problem would have*

been the installation of pneumatic caissons, a costly and time-consuming process, to seal off the quicksand.

"We elected instead to try the chemical soil solidification," said Mr. Fisher. "It's never been used in a project like this before but we were sure we'll be able to form a wall five or six feet thick of sandstone between the quicksand and our excavation.

"The chemical process duplicates nature, but nature would take a couple of million years. We couldn't wait that long."

Now, how can that story you have just read be used to build strong and successful men and women out of weak failures? As the engineers poured a solution of sodium silicate and calcium chloride into quicksand to make solid stone, so we "pour," via sermons and books and speeches, positive spiritual and mental ideas into the negative and defeated minds of people. An idea dropped into such a mind can (and I've often seen this miracle happen) change a weak, irresolute failure into a strong, brilliant success.

Take Charles Kennard, for example. He was at heart a good fellow and had the makings of a strong, successful person. He was a salesman and had a brilliant record in sales—until he became an alcoholic. Finally he lost so much time from the job that his president called him in and said, "Charles, you were far and away the best salesman we ever had until you became a drunk. I hate to say this, but unless you can control your drinking, we're going to bite the bullet and let you go." He told Charles this two additional times. The third time he got really tough and said, "This is the last time. You are out if you don't take steps."

So Charles went to New York to see one of the greatest authorities on alcoholism, Dr. Silkworth. He was drunk when he reached New York and showed too much money when he tipped the bellboy in the hotel. During the night he was robbed, and the next morning he had just about enough to pay his hotel bill.

Dr. Silkworth admitted him to his hospital and two weeks later said, "Charles, we have got you entirely free of alcohol. You were loaded with it when you arrived. But I cannot reach that place in your mind that forms reservations, so you will be back for the same treatment until . . ."

"Until what?" Charles asked.

The doctor shrugged.

"But, Doctor," Charles protested, "you are known to be the greatest healer of alcoholism, and you are saying you can't heal me. Who then can?"

The doctor said, "There is a Doctor who can for sure heal you, but He is terrifically expensive."

"Oh, whatever the cost—I've got money."

"No, you don't understand. This Doctor does not care about money. He wants you—everything you are. He wants all of you."

"Well," shouted Charles, "give me his name and address. I am a total failure unless I'm healed of this disease."

Dr. Silkworth stood up and very impressively said, "This Doctor is a genius. He can read into the mind of a patient and skillfully exorcise even the desire for alcohol. You want His name and address. Well, His name is Jesus Christ and He keeps office in the New Testament. Go to Him, give yourself to Him, and He can heal you for sure and forever."

Charles was impressed, and he went out to walk along the city streets.

He had no idea where he might find "Dr. Jesus," and he did not know the name of any church, nor a pastor. Charles was a Presbyterian in Virginia. Then suddenly he thought of me because he had read *The Power of Positive Thinking*. But he did not remember the name of the church. So he asked a policeman.

By now it was about eleven o'clock at night, and it was snowing and getting colder. He found the church and tried every door, but they all were locked. But there was a mail slot in a side door at the back.

Charles fished in his pocket for his business card, and on the back of it he wrote the following: "Dear Dr. Jesus: I am your unfaithful servant Charles Kennard. I've been told by a great doctor that You alone can heal me. I hereby give You myself, everything, holding nothing back. Please heal me. Thank You. Charles Kennard." He shoved the card through the mail slot.

Standing on the doorstep, the snow pelting down upon him, he suddenly had a warm feeling come over him from head to foot. Alternately he laughed and cried. Then suddenly, he said in telling me about this experience, "I knew I was healed the same way Jesus healed people in the Bible."

I encountered Charles at places where I was speaking, and once I noticed he was nervous. So I bought a pack of postcards and gave them to him with the request that he send me a card every day saying, "Another dry day," and to sign it. The cards kept coming regularly for two or three weeks, then stopped. I let two days go by and telephoned to ask why. He said, "An amazing thing happened. I have lost the desire."

Later I hired him away from his business in Staunton, Virginia, to be the southern representative for *Guideposts* magazine, and I know he was permanently healed of his old trouble. Today he is loved in memory all over the southland.

All through the eighties inventions and improvement of previous inventions described in earlier chapters were still coming from the ingenious minds of Americans, which leads us to the conclusion that mechanisms not yet thought of and refinements of existing inventions, themselves miraculous by our present standards, will come in the twenty-first century, soon to dawn. The inventive mind is still very much alive in the United States.

In 1982 the economy was in recession, interest rates remaining high. The jobless rate, at 10.4 percent, reflected more people out of work than at any time since the Great Depression of the thirties. But as in the thirties this was a worldwide situation.

A wedding was held on July 29, 1981, which was watched on TV with great interest worldwide. It was the wedding of Prince Charles, next king of England, to Lady Diana Spencer in St. Paul's Cathedral, London. The ceremony was performed by the archbishop of Canterbury. The newly married couple drove through admiring throngs to Buckingham Palace. They rode in a seventy-year-old gilded, horse-drawn carriage on which was a hand-scrawled Just Married sign, a nice little informal touch making them seem more like everyone else.

A new national newspaper made its debut on September 15, 1982. It was called *USA Today* and was founded by my friend Allen Neuharth. It had a full page in color reporting weather conditions all over the nation. It was destined to achieve enormous success and indeed to become a world newspaper, having some foreign editions.

In 1922, DeWitt and Lila Wallace had begun mimeographing articles that impressed and interested them and sent copies to friends. Sixty years later, in 1982, the Wallaces' *Reader's Digest* had become the world's largest publishing empire with over 30 million subscribers in many countries, 18 million in the United States. Mr. and Mrs. Wallace were given the Presidential Medal of Freedom by President Nixon.

In 1983 the city of Chicago elected its first black mayor, Mayor Harold Washington. Dr. Sally Ride became the first woman to go into space. As the *Challenger* took off, onlookers appropriately chanted, "Ride, Sally, Ride." President Reagan declared the Soviet government an "evil empire." The U.S. Marine headquarters in Lebanon was destroyed by a bomb containing three hundred pounds of TNT. The suicide driver of the truck containing the bomb killed more than 240 people. The decade produced a mixture of social justice gains and social ills, but always some advancement. Humanity seems to have to move forward through peril, toil, and pain, but go forward it does.

As Christmas 1983 came on, my wife, Ruth, came up with a plan: we would take our children, their spouses, and our eight grandchildren to Jerusalem and the Holy Land and celebrate the birth of Christ where it occurred, in Bethlehem. It would be a memory for the grandchildren to carry through life. Accordingly, the entire Peale family flew to Amman, Jordan, to see the great ruins there, then up to Jerusalem. At every place where Jesus was reported to have been, a member of our family party, old or young, would read the biblical story from a Bible that Ruth had previously supplied everyone. We were literally following in the footsteps of Jesus.

On Christmas Eve we attended a service arranged by the Jerusalem YMCA. It was held in the Shepherd's Fields where "there were in the same country shepherds abiding in the field, keeping watch over their flock by night," at exactly the same historic spot where these humble men heard the sublime announcement, "Unto you is born this day in the city of David a Saviour, which is Christ the Lord."

It was cold that night in the Shepherd's Field, but several thousand believers were there, held spellbound by the place and the night. A great, full, silvery moon rose over the mountains, and in its light everything stood out so clearly that we caught ourselves half expecting that once again the heavens would open "and suddenly a multitude of the heavenly host" would be "praising God and saying, Glory to God in the highest, and on earth peace, good will toward men."

After the service concluded, we said in the words of the shepherds, "Let us now go even to Bethlehem," which we could see on a hill hardly a mile away. There we joined a multitude of pilgrims from all over the world to see the spot where Jesus was born. Standing there, Ruth read aloud the story of the Savior's birth as written by St. Luke.

The next morning, Christmas Day, we had an opening of gifts in our suite in the American Colony Hotel in Jerusalem, where we had stayed many times in the past.

For me, perhaps the most impressive moment of this family pilgrimage to the Holy Land to walk where Jesus walked was the hour spent at the place where Jesus gave the Sermon on the Mount. A gentle hillside rises from the Sea of Galilee, the blue waters lying serene and unruffled below hills beyond. Some of the family sat on the ground, a few on benches under the trees, while our son, John Stafford Peale, Ph.D., a professor of philosophy at Longwood College in Virginia, read the entire Sermon on the Mount, which is recorded in St. Matthew, chapters 5, 6, and 7. Most of us have often heard portions of it read in church, but I had never before heard it in its entirety at one reading.

As John thoughtfully read this immortal document under the trees on the hillside, where a great audience had heard it delivered the first time by the Master Himself, the thought came to me that I was hearing the basic principles of free civilization—and the greatest summary of the principles of meaningful and happy living on earth. The scene and the uplifted thought will, I believe, live with all of us forever, and I hope that we will live sincerely by the commonsense rules laid down in the greatest speech of all time.

Jesus Christ's teachings are practical and sensible, and they work, as the following letter indicates.

Dear Dr. Peale:

As one of your longtime fans, I've wanted to write you for years, but have never taken the time. Today I'm taking time!

I'd like to relate to you what a difference PMA (Positive Mental Attitude) has had in my life. I began listening to this type of material while driving and then branched out to books. Of all the tapes I have (hundreds), yours are favorites. I think it's because of the "Christian influence" in your messages. So many other speakers and authors fail to connect PMA with God. I've read many of your books and subscribe to Guideposts and PLUS magazines.

I have never been a negative person per se, but realized that occasionally I need to be "revitalized." Doesn't everyone? Oh, sure, I still get down, but your stories and sermons seem to pull me up and keep me going.

Your inspiration has truly been a positive force in my life. About the time I started reading and listening to you, my business exploded. In the last six years (since I started listening to PMA) I have a successful business, net worth over one million, a lovely wife, and three lovely children (and a great church family!). All at age 37. It's amazing to me, but I have to give credit to you and your fascinating material.

What a wonderful life you have had and what a great impact you have made on people like me.

Keep up the good work, Doc. Give my best to Ruth!

Sincerely,
Greg Henson

In March of 1984 I was on a speaking tour that took me far afield. I was preparing for another busy day when the telephone rang in my hotel room in Los Angeles. It was a call from Doris Phillips, my longtime secretary in our office in New York. She was calling to tell me that she had just taken a call from the White House and that she had accepted an invitation for me to go there on March 26. "Don't put another date on your schedule for that day," Doris said.

"What's up?" I asked.

"You are to be awarded the Presidential Medal of Freedom," Doris replied.

"Are you kidding me, Doris?" I asked. "Do you know that is the highest award a president can give to a civilian?"

"Now, Dr. Peale, you know I wouldn't give anything but the facts about such a distinction. Congratulations!"

I hung up the receiver and sat there, stunned. Then the faces of my deceased mother and father came to me. They would be so pleased that one of their sons was to be honored by our president at the White House with the great Presidential Medal of Freedom. I thought of how they sacrificed and denied themselves that their three boys could have a good education. I must admit that as I thought of them, I was deeply moved. Tears welled up in my eyes.

Perhaps the presentation ceremony on March 26 would be of interest to readers. The awardees and their families met for luncheon in the East Room. Among them were Senator Howard H. Baker, Jr., of Tennessee, majority leader of the United States Senate; James Cagney, noted actor; Leo Cherne from Tennessee, famous entertainer; Denton Cooley, M.D., heart surgeon; Hector P. García, M.D.; General Andrew J. Goodpaster; and Lincoln Kirstein, ballet master. There was also Louis L'Amour, the greatest writer of westerns since Zane Grey. I told him that I was one of his fans.

The president honored Jackie Robinson, great baseball player, posthumously. The award was received by Jackie's widow. Other posthumous awards went to President Anwar Sadat of Egypt, received by his son, and Eunice Kennedy Shriver, sister of the late president; also, an award was posthumously given to Whittaker Chambers.

One by one the awardees came forward to be greeted by President and Mrs. Reagan. The president read a citation and gave each one the coveted award.

My citation read as follows:

With a deep understanding of human behavior and an appreciation for God's role in our lives, Dr. Norman Vincent Peale helped originate a philosophy of happiness. Through the American Foundation of Religion and Psychiatry and his many books, Dr. Peale became an advocate of the joy of life, helping millions find new meaning in their lives. Few Americans have contributed so much to the personal happiness of their fellow citizens as Dr. Norman Vincent Peale.

It was signed, Ronald Reagan.

Naturally, I appreciated this generous statement by the president. He is a man of utmost kindness; this is why he is so universally loved.

The day before the award presentation and luncheon, President Reagan gave his State of the Union address to the combined Senate and House of Representatives, in which he said, "America is back—standing tall, looking to the eighties with courage, confidence, and hope." On November 6 Ronald Reagan won a monumental victory in the 1984 reelection campaign, carrying forty-nine states, to one by former Vice President Walter Mondale. Mr. Reagan campaigned on the slogan It's Morning Again in America. George Bush was reelected vice president.

In 1985 Montgomery Ward announced that after 113 years, it was dropping its catalog. It was an institution when I was a small boy in Cincinnati. Montgomery Ward was founded in a livery stable in 1872 with $2,400 capital.

The country was devastated on January 28, 1986, when the space shuttle *Challenger* exploded in a massive fireball seventy-eight seconds after lift-off, killing all seven astronauts aboard. The crowd of spectators gathered for lift-off included many students of Christa McAuliffe of Concord, New Hampshire, who was to have been the first schoolteacher in space.

Sadly, the eighties was the decade in which a few prominent TV evangelists were disgraced in scandals, and one actually went to prison. While sadness is felt over the fall of outstanding and gifted leaders of Christianity, we are thankful for all the sincere, self-sacrificing, honest men and women who compose the clergy in America. They never get their names in the papers, for they spend their days simply doing good. Because they are of such sincerity, they are considered not newsworthy, for news is essentially a departure from the norm.

These men and women are always dealing with human problems, many of which are exceedingly complex. An important factor in knowing yourself and therefore liking yourself is to respect yourself. Self-esteem is vital to being successful as a person. Tennyson said, "Self-reverence, self-knowledge, self-control—these three alone lead life to sovereign power."

Self-esteem is one quality the personality simply cannot do without. It has long roots into the ego itself and, in fact, is actually related to fundamental identity. And to have one's basic identity depreciated, especially by yourself, is perhaps the greatest of all blows to the personality. Deep within human nature is a basic sense of sacredness regarding one's person. Most people do not think of this in quite such dramatic terms, for there is a warped tendency these days to think of sacredness as "corny." But even so, there is a point of basic human dignity in every person that must never be offended. This is that inner area of consciousness where the divine Spirit resides in you. If this is violated, it does extraordinary and serious damage to the individual. When this happens to a person, he or she suffers the most painful form of self-dislike, and, as a result, the personality deteriorates.

Let me tell you of a human drama of the eighties, one that illustrates how loss of self-esteem may bring on an acute self-dislike, so acute that it can lead to attempted self-destruction.

Happily, the story also contains a positive cure. I believe it will mean more to you if I let this woman tell the story in her own words, just as she wrote it for *Guideposts* magazine. It is anonymous, of course.

It was autumn; the hills around the town where we lived flamed with scarlet and gold. But I was past caring about the season. All through the long, hot summer, a sense of guilt and unworthiness had been festering in me. The reason had a stark simplicity. The previous spring I had done something wrong. I had been unfaithful to my husband.

My husband didn't know. No one knew, except the other man . . . and I was no longer seeing him. I hated myself. I went to church. I prayed. I asked God to forgive me. But I could not forgive myself.

I said nothing to anyone; I was too ashamed. But I was not so sure that the man in the case was being equally silent. I began to imagine that a certain coolness had appeared in some of my friends. I thought I sensed an aloofness in our mother. I became sure my guilty secret was a secret no longer.

As the summer wore on, my morbid imaginings grew more acute. On my birthday, I remember, someone sent me a greeting card with best wishes for "a happy occasion." The letter a happened to be capitalized and printed in red ink. To me it was the scarlet letter: A for Adulteress. I tore up the card with trembling fingers.

My upbringing had left me with a stern and demanding conscience—too stern, perhaps too demanding. Now my reason, my sense of values, everything was crumbling under its relentless pressure. I could not think—I could only feel. I lost weight. I could not sleep.

My husband urged me to see a doctor, but I refused. I was beginning to think that my husband also knew my secret and was afraid that if I went to the doctor, he, too, would know, would do or say something to reveal his conviction that I was unworthy, unclean, unfit to be a wife or mother. I lived in hell, a hell of my own making.

It was something my husband said that triggered my final act. He was reading in the newspaper about some woman who had deserted her family, had run off with another man. "Good riddance," he said. "They'll be better off without her!"

I felt the icy fingers inside me tighten; my husband was telling me that he knew my secret—and that he wanted to be rid of me.

There can be a terrifying logic in a disordered mind. The woman who had run away with her lover, I reasoned, was more honest and less hypocritical than I. My husband thought she deserved to lose her family. What punishment, then, should be meted out to me, whose whole life had become a lie? I asked myself this with agonized intensity, and somewhere inside of me a voice seemed to answer like a muffled bell tolling: "You're no good to anyone. You're bringing disgrace on your family. You ought to remove yourself altogether. Then they could start a new life, without you."

Without a word to anyone, I went upstairs and packed a small suitcase. I took a length of string and lowered it to the ground from the bedroom window. I came back downstairs, walked past my husband, went into the kitchen, let myself out the back door. I went downtown and registered under an assumed name in the town's tallest hotel.

My room was on the fifth floor. I was afraid it wouldn't be high enough. I walked to the window and looked down. The street below was dark, but I could see the lights of the traffic. I was terrified of dying, but the voice inside was louder, now, fierce, inexorable, telling me that I was unfit to be a member of the human race.

I sat down at the desk and wrote a note to my husband, telling him that I loved him and the children, but that things would be better this way. I wept as I wrote it, but I wrote it. The voice kept telling me to hurry, hurry. I opened the window and closed my eyes; I didn't dare look down. "O God!" I said out loud, and turned around and sat down on the sill, and let myself fall backward into the empty darkness.

I fell five stories; I waited for the impact of the pavement, for nothingness, for oblivion. Instead I smashed into the top of a parked convertible. I went through the canvas roof, into the back seat. I felt an agonizing pain in my back and legs. Then I fainted.

I came to in a quiet hospital room. I tried to move and couldn't. I was encased in plaster from the waist down. A man in a white coat was looking down at me. Quite a young man, with steady, sympathetic eyes. "I'm your doctor," he said. "How are you feeling?"

A wave of despair washed over me. I was still alive, such a miserable bungler that I had failed even to do away with my-self. Even death wouldn't have me. I felt hot tears sting my eyes. "O God," I said. "God forgive me!"

The young doctor put his hand on my forehead. "He will," he said calmly. "Don't worry about anything. We're going to help you learn to love yourself again."

Love yourself again. I never forgot those words; they were the key that opened the door of the prison of self-hate that I had built around myself. They contained the truth that ulti-mately made it possible for me to rebuild my life.[2]

That is an extreme case of a person who hated herself so much that she could no longer tolerate herself. Fortunately, not many suffer so acutely. But vast numbers of people are afflicted with a similar personality problem in less degree. They are not right within themselves, and, as a result, they have lost much of the pleasure they once had in living with themselves.

But there is no need for anyone to continue in this unhappy condition of mind. The way out is, first, to want out, and second, to get some help from a good counselor, a minister, a spiritually wise friend, maybe a doctor or a psychiatrist, the latter if he has spiritual understanding. If he hasn't, don't touch him with a ten-foot pole.

Third, do some real basic praying, of the kind that calls upon the saving grace of Jesus Christ your Savior. Just tell the Lord honestly that you are fed up with yourself and don't want to be as you are anymore. Tell Him you can't seem to do anything really constructive about yourself and so you are turning to Him to do with you just what you need. God will always answer an honest, humble, and trusting prayer of that quality. He will set in motion in you that creative three-point process: self-releasing,

[2] Marguerite C——, "Love of Self," *Guideposts*, April 1960.

self-finding, self-esteeming. Then you will start liking yourself again.

One of the top stories of the eighties is of the flight to Hawaii of Ferdinand Marcos, for many years president of the Philippines, and the elevation to that office of Cory Aquino, widow of the murdered Benigno. She proved a wise and strong head of state. Ferdinand Marcos is now deceased, and a U.S. court has acquitted Mrs. Marcos of any charges against her.

In an earlier chapter we told of the so-called unsinkable ship, the *Titanic*, which struck an iceberg in the North Atlantic on its maiden voyage in 1912 and sank, carrying more than fifteen hundred passengers to death. Divers using undersea robots equipped with TV cameras reported finding the sunken ship in 1985, seventy-three years after she sank. The ship rests at a depth of twelve thousand feet of water. The exact location is not divulged for fear of looters. The sinking of the *Titanic* on an April night was the big news story of my youth. So the finding of the gigantic luxury liner on the bottom of the sea nearly seventy-five years later seems an appropriate bridge spanning the incredible twentieth century.

On May 31, 1988, I became ninety years of age. Ruth, abetted by many friends, had a big party in the Grand Ballroom of the Hotel Waldorf Astoria. It was packed with friends from all over the United States and Canada, some even from overseas.

Phyllis George Brown, Mrs. John Y. Brown, was Master of Ceremonies and was as beautiful and competent as always. Former governor of Kentucky John Y. Brown and the Donald Trump family were sponsors of the dinner.

Charming speeches were made by Bernadette Castro, head of the Castro Convertible Company. President Ronald Reagan, who was out of the country for a summit meeting with Mr. Gorbachev, had made a film in which he graciously extended birthday greetings. Our son, Dr. John Stafford Peale, made a deeply affecting talk about his father and mother.

After all these friends had spoken so kindly, I came on and tried to respond fittingly, but Ruth really "stole the show" with her beautiful speech. The honor guest of the occasion dwindled into insignificance when compared with the brilliant and moving remarks of his wife of nearly sixty years.

Next day at Pawling the beautiful new Center for Positive Thinking building was dedicated by my dear friend, the one and only Art Linkletter, in a characteristically humorous and wonderful speech. The chairman of the dedication ceremonies was John M. Allen, chairman of the board of the Foundation for Christian Living, and as usual he captivated the big audience with his wit.

So I reached ninety years, and we opened another beautiful building and put the capstone on nine decades of an exciting life.

CHAPTER 10

The Nineties: Decade of Freedom

A S I finish writing this book in the fall of 1990, the decade of the nineties is not yet a year old. But the past few months will surely go reverberating down through the history of the world. For in the last months of 1989 and the first months of 1990 Communism proved to be the gigantic flop of the ages, and the world vigorously repudiated it.

Uncounted thousands of shouting men and women in the cities of Eastern Europe surged through the streets and, in famous public squares, raised the cry "We want freedom."

For at least forty years they had been ruled by Communism in one secularized state after another until their economic systems had worn thin, while the free West lived, generally, in prosperity and plenty. With Christianity outlawed for decades, the moral structure of Communistic countries had deteriorated. Their lives in shambles, the people of those ancient states rose en masse to abolish Communism and embrace democracy and religion. The world surely will emerge into a new level of improvement because of the events at the conclusion of this incredible century.

These history-making, almost simultaneous uprisings in country after country were like nothing that had ever before occurred in the history of the human race.

Perhaps one of the best accounts of the 1989 and 1990 worldwide uprising against Communism was written by David Aikman, foreign affairs correspondent for *Time* magazine. In *Christian Herald* magazine, Mr. Aikman writes:

> *It was a stunning moment. I stood on the main balcony about 100 feet from the speakers' platform, overlooking 600,000 Czechoslovakians—the second largest protest crowd in Czech history. They had come to the Sunday rally at the Letna Parade Ground overlooking Prague to hear speakers demand reform. Many jumped up and down to keep warm in the sub-freezing cold, which froze the ink in my ballpoint pen as I tried to take notes.*
>
> *The speakers' overall mood was militantly political in these waning days of Communist rule. Then Vaclav Maly, a Roman Catholic priest, stood to address the crowd.*
>
> *"Let's say The Lord's Prayer," Maly said. The crowd fell silent, uncertain how to cope with this public display of religion. As Maly began, much of the crowd followed, reciting—or trying to recite—a prayer unuttered in public gatherings in more than 40 years.*
>
> *The demonstration was one of a series that swept through Czechoslovakia in late November [1989]. For several days before the Sunday rally hundreds of thousands of people gathered in Prague's Wenceslas Square to voice their opposition— not only to Communism, but to the moral system Communism brought with it.*
>
> *At a Wenceslas Square rally, thousands chanted for "Free elections! Free elections!" as speakers urged reform. Then Josef Hromadka, a prominent protest figure who'd suffered considerably for his faith, began to address the excited crowd.*
>
> *"We live in a society that's sick and needs a remedy," Hromadka said. "Remember the figure of Jesus Christ. Our long history is full of Christianity. Let's look at this history, and take note of its value."*
>
> *The crowd was quiet, nobody cheered. People didn't seem to*

know what to make of this religious expression in a secular-
ized society. But during the 10 days it took to topple the Com-
munist regime, Christians kept pointing the crowds to
something more than a mere change of government.
   Despite decades of Communist attempts to stamp out reli-
gion, the democratic revolutions of Eastern Europe
reconfirmed one of the oldest lessons of Christian history:
When secular tyrannies try to destroy God's people and his
kingdom, the tyrannies are destroyed.[3]

Few of us living in the incredible twentieth century ever
thought that in our lifetime we would see an article in an
American newspaper such as appeared in the *Los Angeles Times*
on September 9, 1990; the headline in large type read: "Out-
rage Over Bread Shortages Undermining Support for Soviet
Reforms."

People are left without bread. It is a terrifying sentence for a
nation that lives on bread, that has come to consider it the one
dependable product in the midst of an economy gone haywire
that sees it, as it has throughout history, as the symbol of well-
being, even of life itself.
   For a Russian, a meal without bread is considered no meal
at all, and that quick stop in the neighborhood bread store for
a couple of loaves to put on the family table has been a central
ritual of Soviet daily life for decades.
   The steady supply of bread was an unwritten but inviolable
Communist covenant with the people. No matter what hap-
pens, the party told them, you will always have bread: you
will never go hungry again.
   "How can this be?" [asked] an outraged pensioner standing
in line the other day at the capital's premier bread store.
"They bring in a great harvest, and there's no bread in the
store. Soon the windows in all the bread stores will be shat-
tered," he predicted. "The people will rise up."
   As Gorbachev prepares to launch a radical new economic pro-
gram, and Moscow readies equally daring plans to turn the city

---

[3] David Aikman, "The Dove and the Axe," *Christian Herald*, May/June 1990.

into an island of virtual capitalism, the bread shortage is costing the reformers in power desperately needed public confidence.

On July 19, 1990, Ruth and I went to Yorba Linda, California, at the invitation of former president Richard Nixon, to participate in the dedication of the beautiful and magnificent Richard Nixon Library and Birthplace. Four presidents attended this ceremony, which was an unusual and impressive occasion. President Bush, President Nixon, President Reagan, and President Ford were present, together with their wives. All the presidents made thoughtful and appropriate speeches. Dr. Billy Graham opened the program with prayer, and I closed it with a prayer of benediction. Ruth and I were seated with the presidential party on the platform, facing many thousands in the audience.

That night a black tie celebration dinner was held in the Grand Ballroom of the Century Plaza Hotel in Los Angeles, at which Ruth and I were at the head table. I had the honor of speaking, together with President Nixon, former Ambassador to Britain Walter Annenberg, and former cabinet officers in a gala and unforgettable occasion attended by a large audience of famous personages. Repeated references were made to the "unparalleled phenomenon of freedom" resurging in the ancient states of Eastern Europe. The twentieth century, the incredible century, was closing in glory.

In writing about the great 1990s, I would just say that we average citizens are going on with our lives. So I want to comment on a question that is often asked me. A reporter asked it recently after hearing me speak to an audience of three thousand. "How can you, at age ninety-two, talk for forty-five minutes with all that energy, enthusiasm, and gestures?"

My answer was direct and simple: "That is the way I have always spoken. And I'm still the same person I have always been. I am still interested, enthusiastic, and concerned about human affairs." I thank God that I have lived to see the world-wide collapse of Communism.

Another question often asked is: "How does one have such good health, energy, and mental clarity at age ninety-two?"

I'm certainly no oracle on the scientific subject of aging, but I am glad to share my views on how one may prolong creative years and have good health.

When I was about sixty-five years old, I was the speaker at a convention luncheon of one of America's big industries in the old Sherman Hotel that stood at the corner of Clark and Randolph Streets in Chicago's "Loop." At the time, it was one of the most famous of hotels and handled huge conventions.

The hotel was operated by two brothers, Frank and Gus Bering, friends of mine, both now deceased. They had grown up in the village of Lynchburg, Ohio, where my parents were also reared. Both Frank and Gus had a nostalgic loyalty to Lynchburg and always extended complimentary room and meal service to me as an "old Lynchburg boy." Naturally, I always stayed in their hotel.

Seated at the head table at this luncheon, I noticed Frank making the rounds of the large dining room to see that every-thing was in order. I admired him very much, for I knew that Frank, at eighty-seven years of age, was running this large and important hotel. So I said admiringly, "Frank, how old are you, anyway?" to which he answered, "What's the matter? Aren't your room and meals OK?"

"Sure are," I replied. "Anyway, I know how old you are, for you went to school with my mother. You are eighty-seven."

He punched me in the chest (and it was no gentle tap), which I knew was his way of expressing affection. He said, "Son [and that "son" went over big with me], let me tell you something which will be of value when you grow up. Live your life and forget your age." So saying, he went energetically about his business. But he had said an important bit of wisdom: "Live your life and forget your age." I have done that ever since.

The man sitting next to me asked, "Is Mr. Bering really eighty-seven?" and concluded, "He's a wonder."

That evening, as I had dinner with Frank and Gus in the hotel, Frank said, "When I look in the mirror I never see an old man. I see Frank Bering, period!"

I also adopted that philosophy of life: "When I look in the mirror I never see a man of ninety-two. I see Norman Vincent Peale, period, just as he has always been."

My own rules of health include always thinking health, always seeing myself as in good health, praying with continuous affirmations of well being. I think the type of thoughts Jesus teaches. I go early to bed and rise early, always putting complete trust in the Lord. I love people, hate no one, eat moderately, and never smoke or drink liquor. I trust God's providence, practice positive thoughts, and live by faith attitudes. And I'm no saint. I just try to be a practicing Christian at all times.

I am certain that these ideas and practices have much to do with the fact that at ninety-two I am in good health. I am grateful to God my heavenly Father. I am in His hands—but He gave me a mind and expects me to use it. And I believe, as do many scientists, that right thinking can have powerful results.

I have read *Meditations* by Marcus Aurelius for years. He says, "I affirm that tranquility is nothing else than the good ordering of the mind. Constantly, then, give to thyself this retreat, and renew thyself." And I believe Professor William James, father of American psychological science, was right in saying, "The greatest discovery of my generation is that a human being can alter his life by altering his attitudes of mind."

I have made effective use of my imagination. You can "see" yourself in a healthy state rather than holding thoughts of sickness and disintegration. I think of myself as God's creation and affirm that the Creator is also the Re-creator when anything goes amiss. And I believe also that the subconscious is our friend and willing servant and wants to give us what we want, namely, health. Therefore imagination, affirmation, and faith are powerful factors in finding health. Many medical doctors attest to the importance of a patient's upbeat, optimistic attitude while combatting even a serious disease.

Deep breathing, mastery of inner conflict, faith in God, picturing the good, positive thoughts, and implicit belief are all good assistants of your doctor in producing health and longevity. Health is the gift of God in cooperation with yourself. I cannot believe that He intended us to be victimized by fear or by troubles. Psalm 34 says in verse 4, "I sought the Lord, and he heard me, and delivered me from all my fears." Not from most of them, not from some, but from all fears, it plainly says.

As we read the all-out promises of God, we can believe that the Father, the good, loving God, wants us to have health and a long happy life, free from the devastation of fear and trouble.

Tension, stress, fear, and trouble, too, can be controlled by prayer and an attitude of faith, as many have demonstrated. I believe any methodology for good health may be used that produces results and is in harmony with biblical precepts.

In the early chapters of this book I told what we did not have in my youth: electric lighting, indoor plumbing, bathtubs, TV, radio, and automobiles. And we now have all of those and many more. But there's one thing we had in 1900 and 1910 and in every decade since. We have it in 1990 also, and that is trouble. Mankind has always had trouble. Indeed, "Man is born unto trouble as the sparks fly upward" (Job 5:7).

We have also had the way out of trouble, and we have it now. It is stated in Psalm 34, verse 6: "This poor man cried, and the Lord heard him, and saved him out of all his troubles." Not some of them, not even most of them, but the Lord will free us from all of them.

These important verses have helped me all my life.

I believe faith offers a wonderful way to upgrade and improve our lives, and many who have become believers agree. For example, consider the following excerpt from a letter:

> *Dear Dr. Peale,*
>
> *I wanted to write to you to say thank you for all you have done for me. I have been reading your books and pamphlets for more than ten years. Over four years ago I went to treatment for alcoholism. I have been sober ever since. I met a wonderful man who is also a recovering alcoholic. We have had a marvelous marriage for over two years.*
>
> *I believe Bob is my husband due to some of your literature. Several years ago I read about praying for a husband. I did this for a long time. I asked God to send someone to me who believed in God and would love me. Bob is a better husband than I could ever have imagined. We are friends as well as lovers and we help each other daily. Marriages that include God are destined for success. I didn't realize when I began praying for a husband that I would have to go through treatment first. But God always knows what is best.*
>
> *P. L.*

The children of this generation could be free of trouble that they bring upon themselves in the morning of their lives. Some encounter trouble far too early, before they have learned how to deal with it. I have had the experience of speaking to a number of national or state conventions of educators, including elementary teachers and principals. In personally talking with these teachers and administrators at various conventions, I have heard many express the opinion that while children are born with positive attitudes, a high percentage (some place it at 80 percent) have become negative in their thinking and attitudes by the fourth or fifth grade.

To counteract this situation, some of my associates have developed a program called the Power of Positive Students (POPS). It is designed to teach our children the principles of positive thinking and living. Several states are already using POPS effectively in their elementary schools.

What we call POPS is a program for kindergarten to fourth grade. It presents the skills necessary to develop a positive attitude. It is a semester-long program and contains two videos for classroom use, two audios for teachers, a training manual, and written support materials for teachers and parents.

Classroom teachers have identified the greatest threats to the educational process as they were perceived fifty years ago contrasted with those of the present. This shocking comparison was published by the Fullerton, California, Police Department and the California Department of Education in February of 1988.

1940	TODAY
1. Talking out of turn	*1. Drug abuse*
2. Chewing gum	*2. Alcohol abuse*
3. Making noise	*3. Pregnancy*
4. Running in the halls	*4. Suicide*
5. Getting out of line	*5. Rape*

Though I believe we can prevent it from developing, the deterioration of American youth is a real threat. The good news is that research clearly shows that these antisocial, self-destructive behaviors can be traced to a single source—low self-esteem.

The goal of POPS is to restore a healthy sense of self-assurance, elevate levels of self-esteem, and cultivate positive attitudes. The materials we use are a product of teachers, children, and parents working with professional talent. They address self-awareness, goals and expectations, enthusiasm, and coping.

And the program, where used, has already made a difference in the lives of children.

Young viewers of the video program recognize problems similar to their own, and by sharing vicariously in the choice-making process, they learn to deal with these problems in positive, beneficial ways. Audio programming delivers a level of motivation that can be achieved only when peers, teachers, and experts share thoughts, feelings, frustrations, and triumphs with one another. The enthusiasm expressed for this program has been an encouraging impetus to all involved.

POPS Multimedia is being used in a growing number of states. Thus far, more than 650,000 children, with their parents and teachers, have been part of this vital, growing network.[4]

And how may adults handle trouble, the persistent nemesis of the human race? This is a complex and important question. And to be successful is to become a consummate master of the art of living. It is to be an achiever of success and enduring happiness. One of our readers found it so as he states in the following letter:

> *Dear Dr. Peale:*
>
> *Do you remember when you wrote that tremendous book The Power of Positive Thinking?*
>
> *In 1954, we were struggling to make ends meet, but I formed an insurance agency.*
>
> *On that late afternoon in 1954, into my little office came John Randle, vice president of the small bank around the corner. John had just turned me down for a five-hundred-dollar loan the day before. He was serious but affable, and he said: "I want you to get this book, The Power of Positive Thinking; I believe it can do you a lot of good. If you can't spare the cost, I'll loan it to you. You can get this at Cokesbury Book Store, down the street."*
>
> *I went to Cokesbury's immediately and bought the book, and on*

---

[4] For more information about the POPS material write to: Foundation for Christian Living, P.O. Box FCL, Pawling, NY 12564.

*the bus on the way home I had finished reading two chapters.
It had so lifted my spirits that I felt almost like a new man!
That night, Bernice and I sat around the kitchen table, and
she would read a chapter, then I would read a chapter, and we
would discuss what we had read, as you suggested in the book.*

*Well, with the help of the good sense and inspiration con-
tained in that book, we were able to build our faith back
where it belonged. And we worked! Oh, how we worked!*

*We continued to read and discuss The Power of Positive
Thinking, and it helped us to build our faith stronger. In four
years we had paid all our debts. And we began saving money.*

*I am retired. Now here I am at an advanced age, confront-
ing a serious situation. If I don't watch it, I could think myself
into being an invalid!*

*But wait! Common sense comes upon the scene! "Where is
that book, The Power of Positive Thinking?" We searched.
Where is that book? I need that book and I'll find it! I need it
to revitalize the power that it assures me is within me! And if
I can rebuild my faith, I can be OK. And God will help me!*

*Sincerely,
Norval A. Dickey*

But even in the prolific climate of freedom where free choice
prevails, some turned their backs on Jesus Christ or drifted away
from Him and His way of life. They argued that he was no
longer "with it" and that His way was outmoded. Something
called a "new morality" took the place of His value system. But
already many of those who embraced these false ideas have
begun to suspect they made a grievous error. They had it made
financially: two cars in the garage, good income, membership in
the country club; but happiness—where was it? They were
"empty on the inside." Now they are discovering that such
emptiness is a lack of spirituality. Therefore, thousands are
going back to the Giver of peace, joy, and meaning and are being
filled "on the inside." They are happy and excited. They are
successful and contented.

At the stroke of midnight on Tuesday, October 2, 1990, forty-five years after it was carved up in disgrace and defeat, Germany was reunited in a celebration of pealing bells, national anthems, and jubilant blare of trumpets. And at that moment, a copy of the American Liberty Bell, a gift from the United States at the height of the Cold War, tolled from the Town Hall in Berlin, and the black, red, and gold banner of the Federal Republic of Germany rose slowly before the Reichstag, the scarred home of past German parliaments.

This was indeed an historic event and was particularly meaningful to those of us who had seen the dismemberment of the great German Empire forty-five years ago as a result of the deplorable Hitler era and the devastating Second World War. Let us hope that the future of the united Germany will be one of peace and tranquility.

World events are happening so rapidly that a book dealing with current events could remain open forever. But every book must find an ending.

I believe the remainder of the 1990s, the final decade of the incredible twentieth century, will be not only a freedom decade but also the decade in which Jesus Christ will again be as dominant as He was when I began this exciting life of energy and action, which has lasted for nine decades plus. I believe that, for He makes any believer's life meaningful, happy, and exciting—indeed, truly wonderful. And I know that to be a fact, for He has done it for me, one of the least of His followers. I am still looking forward, still excited about life, thanking God for all His blessings, for a brilliant and wonderful wife and a family of whom I'm very proud—and a host of friends I love, among whom I include you.

Thank you for reading this book in which I have rambled through this incredible century. God bless you every day, all the way.

INDEX